# THE MORAL CORPORATION – MERCK EXPERIENCES

Merck and the pharmaceutical industry are headline news today. Controversies over public safety, prices, and the ability of the industry to develop the new drugs and vaccines that society needs have swirled over the United States, Europe, and the developing nations. Roy Vagelos, who was head of research and then CEO at Merck from the mid-1970s through the early 1990s, addresses each of these issues in *The Moral Corporation – Merck Experiences*.

Vagelos highlights his efforts to turn around the Merck laboratories and introduce an entirely novel approach to new drug development. Success with targeted research started Merck on a path that would lead to a series of blockbuster therapies that carried the firm to the top of the global industry in the 1980s and 1990s and Vagelos into the top position at the company. Trained as a physician and scientist, he had to learn how to run a successful business while holding the organization and all of its employees to the highest principles of ethical behavior. He was not always successful. He and his co-author explain where and why he failed to achieve his goals and analyze those initiatives that succeeded.

P. Roy Vagelos is retired Chairman of Merck & Co., Inc.; Chairman of Regeneron Pharmaceuticals Inc.; and Chairman of Theravance Corporation. He and Louis Galambos published *Medicine, Science, and Merck* (Cambridge, 2004).

Louis Galambos is Professor of History at The Johns Hopkins University and the editor of *The Papers of Dwight David Eisenhower*. He is the coauthor of a book on vaccine development, *Networks of Innovation* (Cambridge, 1995), and *Anytime, Anywhere* (Cambridge, 2002), a study of the wireless industry.

# THE MORAL CORPORATION – MERCK EXPERIENCES

P. Roy Vagelos

Louis Galambos

CAMBRIDGE
UNIVERSITY PRESS

HD
9666.9
.M4
V34
2006

CAMBRIDGE UNIVERSITY PRESS
Cambridge, New York, Melbourne, Madrid, Cape Town, Singapore, São Paulo

Cambridge University Press
40 West 20th Street, New York, NY 10011-4211, USA

www.cambridge.org
Information on this title: www.cambridge.org/9780521864558

First published 2006

Printed in the United States of America

A catalog record for this publication is available from the British Library.

Library of Congress Cataloging in Publication Data

Vagelos, P. Roy.
The moral corporation / P. Roy Vagelos, Louis Galambos.
p. cm.
Includes bibliographical references and index.
ISBN-13: 978-0-521-86455-8 (hardback)
ISBN-10: 0-521-86455-0 (hardback)
ISBN-13: 978-0-521-68383-8 (pbk.)
ISBN-10: 0-521-68383-1 (pbk.)
1. Merck & Co. – Management. 2. Pharmaceutical industry – Moral and
ethical aspects – United States. 3. Vagelos, P. Roy. 4. Business ethics.
5. Social responsibility of business. I. Galambos, Louis. II. Title.
HD9666.9.M4V34 2006
338.7′616151092 – dc22 2006002543

ISBN-13 978-0-521-86455-8 hardback
ISBN-10 0-521-86455-0 hardback

ISBN-13 978-0-521-68383-8 paperback
ISBN-10 0-521-68383-1 paperback

# Contents

# Preface

"Man that is born of woman," the Book of Job tells us, "is of few days and full of trouble." Our experiences in business, in science, in government service, and in academic life give us plenty of reasons to affirm Job's insight. The evening news, the morning newspaper, and the Internet provide fresh evidence every day of a troubled world. But we also find cause for hope in the everyday events that don't make it into the media, events that inspire the kind of hope that runs through the New Testament and our study of the moral corporation.

Here is a story of life and leadership in an American multi-national, one of the world's leading pharmaceutical companies, Merck & Co., Inc. Merck and the entire pharmaceutical industry are headline news today – mostly bad news. Controversies over public safety, prices, and the ability of the industry to develop the new drugs and vaccines that society needs are swirling through the United States, Europe, and the developing nations.

Those controversies are not new, and they provide a backdrop for this account of the business career of Roy Vagelos, who was head of research and then CEO at Merck from the mid-1970s through the mid-1990s. His experiences in this vital industry include a long, sometimes painful, but ultimately successful attempt to introduce at the Merck laboratories a novel approach to new drug development. Success with targeted research started Merck on a path that would lead the company to a series of blockbuster therapies and to the very top of the global industry.

Trained as a physician and scientist, Vagelos had to learn how to run a successful multinational business while holding the organization and all of its employees to the highest principles of ethical behavior. He made mistakes and we explain in detail where and why he fell short of his own goals. This is, then, a first-hand look at corporate leadership from the inside out, a book that offers a perspective on gender relations and affirmative action, as well as entrepreneurship.

Students in business schools, their professors, the tens of thousands of people who work in pharmaceuticals, and the millions who use their products, invest in their stocks, or are concerned today about healthcare in America should find something of interest in these pages. There is "trouble" as well as "hope" in this account of two decades in the evolution of an innovative, science-based corporation.

We have drawn upon our earlier book, *Medicine, Science, and Merck* (Cambridge University Press, 2004), in drafting these pages and thus received help, directly or indirectly, from all those acknowledged in the preface to that volume. We would, nevertheless, like to give a special thanks to Cambridge editor, Frank Smith, who encouraged us to write a study focused tightly on Roy

Vagelos' career at Merck and the ethical questions the pharmaceutical industry is facing today. We hope this book will help our readers untangle and debate all of those issues, using history as it should be used, to deepen our understanding of the world in which we live.

Roy Vagelos
Louis Galambos
November 2005

# CHAPTER ONE

# The Puzzle

I WAS THE HEAD OF RESEARCH AND DEVELOPMENT AT Merck & Co., Inc., when two of the company's scientists dropped a puzzle in my lap. The puzzle had an important ethical component, but that was not what concerned the scientists who had come to see me. Bill Campbell was a parasitologist who was involved in the discovery and development of ivermectin, a remarkable substance that was active against the worms that plague livestock as well as household pets. He and Mohammed Aziz, an infectious disease specialist, weren't concerned about cattle or horses, however. They had a more intriguing problem in mind. They wanted to spend some of the company's money to see if ivermectin could be used against the parasite that causes river blindness in people.

Mohammed had a good, firsthand knowledge of the disease. He had worked with the World Health Organization (WHO) in Sub-Saharan Africa, where the black fly breeds in the continent's fast-flowing rivers – hence *river* blindness. The flies pick up a tiny parasite (microfilariae) from infected humans and spread it to others. In the victim's skin, the parasites develop into adult worms that can reach two feet in length. They produce millions of microfilariae that crawl through the skin and produce intolerable itching. Even worse, when they enter the eyes, they cause inflammation and then scarring that leaves the victim blind. As Mohammed and Bill explained, there was a good chance that ivermectin might be the first effective treatment for this terrible disease. The drug, they said, was working against a related parasite that attacks horses.

But there was a catch. At that time, it was estimated that 18 million people were infected in Sub-Saharan Africa alone, and in some West African villages 60 percent of the population over fifty-five years old was already blind. According to WHO's estimates, there were over 100 million people living in areas of Africa and Latin America where they were threatened by the disease.[1] If ivermectin worked, there was bound to be a tremendous demand for it. But there was no way either the people at risk or their governments could pay for the treatment.

That was the first part of the puzzle, and I found it relatively easy to solve by saying "Yes." There was a potential downside for me personally. I hadn't been on the job very long and I was still learning how to promote new drug development in a corporate setting. While we had some big innovations in our pipeline, I was still an unproven rookie in the business world. I would be spending a considerable amount of company money in a field, tropical medicine, that few of us other than Mohammed Aziz knew very well.

Still, I had good reason to be confident of what we could accomplish with ivermectin. Merck & Co., Inc., had an impressive

---

[1] The scientific name of the parasite is *Onchocerca volvulus*, and thus the disease is onchocerciasis (pronounced onco-sir-KI-isis).

long-term track record in new drug development. The year I joined the company (1975), it was spending over $120 million on research and development out of total revenue of almost $1.5 billion. Revenue had increased by 12 percent over the previous year, and Merck was doing particularly well in overseas markets, which accounted for 45 percent of the firm's sales. But CEO Henry Gadsden had become worried – with good cause – about Merck's pipeline of new products, and he had hired me to solve that problem. It was as obvious to me as it was to Mohammed and Bill that even if ivermectin was successful against river blindness, the drug wasn't going to pump up the firm's revenue and make the stockholders happy. So I was being asked to take on some risk for myself and for the laboratories.

Nevertheless, I decided to crawl out on that limb. This decision reflected the fact that I was so new to the business world that I still thought of myself as a physician first, scientist second, and president of an industrial laboratory third. So I didn't hesitate and sent Mohammed and a small group of Merck people to Dakar, Senegal, to find out if ivermectin could indeed control river blindness.

The second part of the puzzle would be more expensive, more risky, and more difficult to solve. But before I faced that problem, Mohammed would have to find out if ivermectin worked against river blindness and I would have to learn how to do an entirely different job at Merck. I would have to become a business leader and would have to rearrange my priorities: I would have to become a corporate leader first, a medical scientist promoting innovation second, and a physician concerned about healing third. Before explaining how that happened, what kind of leader I became, and what Merck decided to do with this new drug, I want to tell you a bit more about myself and my background before I got into the pharmaceutical business.

# CHAPTER TWO

# The Professional Path

M Y LIFE HAS IN MANY WAYS BEEN THE CLASSIC American dream: Poor immigrants come to the United States and work very hard; their children receive an excellent education and lead a better life. Like most such myths, the story has some truth to it, as it certainly does in my case.

I was born just before the start of the Great Depression, in October 1929, in Westfield, New Jersey, where my Greek father and one of his brothers owned a shop that sold candy, ice cream, and snacks. Times were hard for all of us, but I grew up in a family that was extremely supportive, even in the harshest days of the 1930s.

I needed support because in elementary school I was a cutup who entertained the other students – but not, of course, the teachers. They were interested in teaching Pindaros Roy Vagelos (they wouldn't use my nickname, Pindo) to read and write in English, goals that seemed formidable to a first grader who spoke only Greek at home. I was a slow learner. I just wasn't interested in learning. Since my last name begins with a "V," I sat in the back of the class, where it was hard to hear. I got used to not paying attention to the lessons, although I pretended to work when the teacher was watching.

The year 1936, when I was in first grade, was an especially difficult one for my family. My father and his oldest brother owned the Westfield Sweet Shoppe in the center of an affluent bedroom community about an hour's drive from New York City. Like many other Greek immigrants, they had gravitated to the candy and small restaurant business because startup costs were small and they were largely uneducated. They could thrive with minimal English, making up with hard work and warm personalities what they lacked in education and capital.

But the hard times of the 1930s didn't spare Westfield or our family business. When the market collapsed, we lost our house. We moved into an apartment above a drugstore about two miles from Westfield, and I thought my life was coming unhinged. My sister and I changed schools. I lost my room and had to sleep on a sofa in the living room.

I remember it like it was yesterday. My parents, Herodotus and Marianthi, never discussed their financial problems in front of me. But I absorbed every sign of urgency in our family. My father and his older brother tried to keep the Sweet Shoppe going by cutting expenses and working longer hours. My mother, who had stayed home before I entered school, took a job ironing clothes in a laundry. After a full day there, she came home and made elaborate evening dresses for the few women in that part of New Jersey who could still afford them. As soon as we could work, we all helped with the family business. I washed windows and swept out the store. I think I learned more about life from these early experiences in my family than I did in school, where I continued to lag.

I learned a great deal from just being around my father. He taught me something about community and interdependence. Watching him help other members of the family come over from Greece provided important lessons about our responsibilities to others. I also learned something about endurance and optimism. Even during the worst years of the Depression, my father considered himself fortunate to be in a place where people could build new lives and had access to greater opportunities for themselves and their children. If you work hard, my father said, you can achieve anything here.

At first, it looked like this lesson was not going to take. I was an able young musician, playing my violin in the school orchestra and singing in the chorus. It encouraged me to think of myself as an entertainer. My father remained gentle but firm. He kept telling me about relatives whose sons had received scholarships to college. He spoke of the advantages of working with a pen behind a desk instead of working long hours on one's feet in a store or a factory.

Gradually, I began to get the picture and started to concentrate more of my energy on schoolwork. Especially when I discovered that mathematics came easily to me. Reading was still a problem. Nevertheless, my academic performance improved steadily, and to my surprise I found myself among the top group of students at Roosevelt Junior High School.

When the economy was recovering in the early 1940s, my father and mother were able to buy the Estelle Luncheonette from another Greek family. So we moved from Westfield to Rahway, a working-class town just five miles away. For me, this move was providential. It threw me into the hands of Miss Brokaw, my high school algebra teacher. Miss Brokaw was young, enthusiastic, and interested in her students. She began to make me feel that I could do something important in life. She constantly challenged me with extra homework assignments, and I responded to that positive pressure by doing exactly what she had in mind.

I also was able to upgrade my position in the family business: Now I was a soda jerk. When I was working the fountain and helping with the tables, I got to know our customers, especially the people who worked for Merck & Co., Inc., which was Rahway's leading business. Merck was only a few blocks from the luncheonette, and many of its scientists and engineers regularly came over for meals. They impressed me with their intelligence and ability to talk about different ideas. The common language seemed to be chemistry, and for the first time I saw people truly excited about the intellectual aspects of their work. I started to see an interesting path opening ahead of me, and it led directly to college, as Miss Brokaw and my father had understood long before I did.

Academic accomplishment brought out a fiercely competitive streak in my personality, something I can't remember having during my early years. I became an honor student on a fast track in science and mathematics, both of which played to my newfound ability in analysis. I was not a geek – the luncheonette prevented that from happening – but I now had all of the energy and determination of a religious convert. My newfound zeal didn't keep me from being turned down when I applied to go to Johns Hopkins, but I had better fortune with the University of Pennsylvania, which became the next leg on my path to a profession.

\* \* \*

I had never even seen the Penn campus before my parents drove me and my single suitcase down to Philadelphia in September 1947 and dropped me at the gate on 37th Street and Woodland Avenue. Beyond the gate were dormitories built around large quadrangles of green lawn. The classrooms and laboratories that absorbed my time over the next three years sprawled on both sides of Woodland Avenue, which divided the campus.

At Penn I found exactly what I was looking for, including the opportunity to set my own pace and to explore what intrigued me. When I found difficult problems to solve in chemistry or physics, problems that sustained my interest, I became even more energized. I learned how to concentrate, to stay focused for longer and longer periods of time. Did the memory of my mother bent over her sewing, my father's long hours in the shop, have anything to do with my drive? I believe they did. Studying late at night, I would recall how hard both my parents worked and reflect on the difference between their lives and those of the professionals who ate at our luncheonette.

The only significant break in my schedule was rowing. I rowed my whole time at Penn with the lightweight crew. I discovered that the discipline of rowing – the physical exertion and team coordination – fit my personality. My teammates became my closest friends. From rowing I learned the benefits of being in peak condition, the importance of teamwork and team leadership, and the positive impact physical fitness could have on my intense studies in chemistry. After I rowed, my concentration was always better.

When I wasn't rowing, I focused with great energy on my studies and was able to graduate in three years. Playing to the hilt my role in the classic American immigrant story, I had become the classic American high achiever. Then, rather suddenly, I had to decide what I was going to achieve after I left Penn. The top two contenders were graduate training in chemistry or medicine. I loved chemistry. Organic chemistry in particular was incredibly exciting to me, and I could see opportunities to make important intellectual and practical contributions through a scientific career.

But inside my head I heard my parents and relatives saying, "You have to do things for others." This was the kind of deeply grooved voice that stays with you for an entire lifetime. Now it guided me away from chemistry and toward medicine. My family was especially proud (as was I) when I was admitted to Columbia University's College of Physicians and Surgeons. Their son was pointed toward an honorable profession, and that was important to the Vagelos clan. The tug-of-war between science and medicine was not over, but for the moment, medicine was the winner.

* * *

Then in the fall of 1950, my triumphant march through academia came to an abrupt halt. Like many other high achievers, I hit a wall. At the College of Physicians and Surgeons (P&S to us), I quickly rediscovered academic anxiety. I found that I was launching my study of the ultimate biology – the anatomy of the human body – with the least possible preparation. What I had mastered at Penn was problem solving in science, my strength, but medical school required memorization, my weakness. I was deeply distressed and uncertain what to do. Returning home at Christmas break, I was on the edge of failing and I contemplated ending my medical career before it began.

Fearful of failure, I returned to New York and ground my way, inch by inch, through anatomy. I survived my first year in medical school, but I had regained some of the humility I seem to have lost at Penn.

I spent the summer after the first year of medical school at home in Rahway working as an intern for Merck & Co., Inc. I would like to claim that the work engaged my imagination, but it wasn't like that at all. Though I had great respect for the company's scientists and I knew that the Merck laboratories were widely respected as a state-of-the-art operation, the rote tasks they assigned me were deadly dull. After that summer, I had no intention of ever returning to Merck or any other pharmaceutical company. The only positive result was to make medical school and a career in medicine look even more attractive.

In my third year at Columbia, I encountered the legendary Dr. Robert F. Loeb, chairman of the Department of Medicine. This towering figure was coauthor of the *Textbook of Medicine* used in many medical schools and revered at Columbia, where it was the bible for both faculty and students. We all studied Loeb's bible with care and also learned a good bit about the author. We knew, for instance, that he had a sadistic streak that emerged when he did medical rounds. Terrified by these encounters, we worked very hard to master the Loeb medical dogma. I survived his rounds relatively unscarred. In fact, I enjoyed clinical medicine so much that I began to set my sights on internal medicine, possibly leading to a specialty in cardiology.

One afternoon toward the end of my fourth year, I was finishing my work in obstetrics and, with no delivery scheduled, I joined the rounds with Dr. Loeb. Most students avoided him after their third year, but I had always done well in his classes, and unfortunately I wasn't afraid. As we stopped at the bed of a patient with inflammation of the kidney, Loeb asked one student after another for the incubation period of the disease. As each confessed ignorance, Loeb's anger mounted. Finally, wheeling to me, he said, "Vagelos, tell these third-year students what *every* P&S student should know!" I had to admit I didn't remember either, and Loeb berated me.

I was stunned at my foolishness in putting myself on Loeb's firing line so casually. Later that day, I walked past Dr. Loeb and his wife and heard him telling her how disappointed he was in me: "This is the person I was telling you about," he said.

\* \* \*

Surviving, again, my next stop on the road to a career took me to Boston, where in 1954, I began my internship in medicine at Massachusetts General Hospital, one of Harvard's teaching hospitals. I felt fortunate to be selected, but as I quickly learned, I was unprepared for the startling transformation from the classroom to the hospital. We were all traumatized at first. We drew together, quickly becoming a tight little community. Each intern formed a team with an assistant resident. The team cooperated closely, sharing all their patients, eating together, and exchanging vital information. We depended on each other.

The fact that I was no longer in medical school came crashing home to me during one of my first solo evenings in charge of a ward. A comatose patient was rushed into the hospital. The emergency room physician told me the patient was thought to be suffering from acute diabetic acidosis, which occurs when blood sugar slips out of control. This can be fatal if not treated promptly. This time I remembered Dr. Loeb's dogma, which told you exactly how to diagnose and treat such cases. Having confirmed the diagnosis, I administered insulin and various intravenous salt solutions. The patient slowly responded, awoke, and began speaking.

I was pleased, but the next morning my medical career suddenly became more complicated. When the assistant resident arrived, the patient was sitting up in bed. The resident said my treatment was quite all right, but he would have done it somewhat differently. I was stunned. The Loeb bible had been questioned. Then the visiting physician said his procedure would have been somewhat different from either mine or the resident's.

Medicine, I realized, is not an exact science. It could not be learned and applied by rote. It required careful analysis of individual situations. Now I was free to think, to use my understanding of basic disease processes and to explore the "art" of medicine. My internship at Mass General broke my faith in the Loeb bible.

My new understanding of medicine helped in the summer and fall of 1955, when Boston suffered a polio epidemic. It was heartbreaking to see hundreds of children and adults stricken. Many of those brought into our wards were partially or completely paralyzed after the virus attacked their central nervous systems. After finishing my internship, I spent the late summer and early fall as the resident in charge of all the adult polio patients who had to be in tank respirators to continue breathing. With thirty to fifty respirators working at one time, it took all of our staff to provide the extra care that was needed. This was my first exposure as a physician to large numbers of people who were completely paralyzed and unable to do anything on their own.

At first, I was profoundly depressed about their plight. There was a terrible feeling of helplessness because we could do nothing to cure their disease and very little to relieve their paralysis. The sense of tragedy was heightened by our awareness that researchers in the United States – most prominently Jonas Salk – were on the verge of producing an effective vaccine against polio.

Teamwork between state and national public health authorities, private foundations, university scientists, and pharmaceutical companies made the field trials of the new vaccine a success in the spring of 1955. I was encouraged to see what cooperation on this level could achieve and to discover during the same months that many of our patients were able to recover to a surprising extent. I learned two lessons: For individuals, I could see that hope plays a significant role in healing; and for society, I recognized that cooperation between the public, nonprofit, and private sectors could play a powerful role in medical innovation.

* * *

I was also learning about the power of teamwork in my personal life, which I was now sharing with my wife, Diana Touliatou. We had and still have much in common. Her parents were also Greek immigrants, and she had been a scholarship student at Barnard who shared my interests in music and sports. There were differences between Diana and me as well. My education was heavily weighted toward science and was relatively narrow. Hers was extremely broad: She majored in economics and history at Barnard and was politically active. In our case these differences didn't pull us apart. Indeed, they made us a strong team.

If we were starting out today, Diana's interests in political science, history, and economics, combined with her college leadership experience, would almost certainly have led her to law school and eventually politics. But back in the 1950s, the combination of Greek and American traditional values, as well as her personal priorities, kept her focused on our family life. My role in that scenario was to focus on a professional career that was just about to experience one of the four decisive changes that would reorder our lives.

* * *

This one involved the ongoing tension between science and medicine that I mentioned before. During the Korean War, I had been deferred from service to complete my medical training, and now I owed the U.S. government two years of military medicine. I enrolled as a medical officer in the U.S. Army, but fate intervened (as my father had told me it would) and I ended up in the U.S. Public Health Service. I was assigned to the National Institutes of Health (NIH) to work as a research physician.

There I encountered my second mentor (remember Miss Brokaw), the distinguished scientist Earl Stadtman. I was just a novice in biochemistry, but Earl swallowed his doubts and allowed me to join his research team at the National Heart Institute. I was the only one without a Ph.D. in biochemistry, so I had plenty of ground to cover if I was not going to disgrace Earl or myself.

Luckily, I landed in a laboratory that was as exciting as it was exacting. By determining biochemical sequences at the molecular level and then characterizing the controlling enzymes, Earl and his fellow scientists were taking a giant step toward understanding life. Learning how to analyze normal – that is, healthy – activities of the cell, they were potentially contributing to a new understanding of how disease altered these biochemical reactions.

Stadtman seemed completely unconcerned about the practical medical implications of what he was doing. His dedication was to basic science. I was intrigued by the basic research, but I was also attracted to the potential applications of enzymology in medicine. I could see that Earl's microbial experiments had the potential to build a new biochemical foundation for modern medicine, and this was a challenge that would reshape my career.

First, I had to learn the basics of research in biochemistry. Earl kindly walked me through the major questions modern biochemists were trying to answer. I was very nervous about my lack of knowledge, but I focused with great intensity on mastering the laboratory techniques and concepts in this rapidly changing discipline.

Part of my training took part in the regular meetings of our "journal club," where we discussed what other scientists in the field were doing. I kept respectfully quiet for a long time, but finally I gained enough confidence to speak up when Earl raised a question. He had very high standards and was a brilliant and outspoken critic of work he didn't like. Sometimes, I even tried to defend the authors against Earl's attacks.

Challenging and intense, Stadtman's biochemistry laboratory was a veritable hothouse for scientific discovery and, in my case, training. The journal club, the lab tutorials with Stadtman, and the lectures by distinguished scientists pulled me, emotionally and intellectually, toward basic research and away from clinical medicine. My obsession with the art of healing didn't disappear, but more and more of my hours were filled with problems issuing from Stadtman. Under his tutelage I was transformed into a research scientist.

\* \* \*

The tension between medicine and science resurfaced as I approached the end of my second year at NIH. Then, Walter Bauer asked me to return to Harvard to join the junior faculty, but Earl encouraged me to stay at NIH. In what for him was a great burst of enthusiasm, he said, "I think you're *pretty good* in biochemistry." "Pretty good" was the strongest compliment he had given me, and I boldly replied: "Well, I'm *very good* at medicine." Earl quickly countered with a proposal: "If you'll stay a third year," he said, "you'll be entirely independent." I accepted that offer and the next day, I discovered what Stadtman meant when he said I would be independent. He stopped talking to me in the laboratory. I had to make my own decisions.

Earl stopped solving my problems, but he didn't stop supporting me. He decided it was time I had a research assistant, and he put me in touch with Al Alberts, two years my junior, who was doing graduate work at the University of Maryland. We quickly agreed to work together. We recognized our differences. He was a great bench scientist with a bulldog determination about getting results. I was more theoretical than Al, better at framing the context for our research. Our skills were complementary – like those of Diana and myself – and Al Alberts and I soon became a smoothly functioning research team.

With four hands instead of two, we accelerated our analysis. In 1959, Al helped me complete my first independent research paper and our project now began to develop its own momentum. Working at the microbial level, we were studying what goes on in cells as they synthesize fat. I believed that our work might some day explain fatty acid synthesis in humans, but that was a distant goal, just a speck on the horizon.

The research quickly became all-consuming, and without Diana's remarkable efforts, our family might have collapsed. Hot science is incredibly demanding. Our family was growing. Randall, our first child, was almost two years old, and his sister Cynthia was born in February 1959. Fortunately, we had found a house within walking distance of NIH so I could pop home quickly for our family dinner. But after dinner, I normally headed back to the laboratory to press on with our explorations of fatty acid biosynthesis.

During my sixth year at NIH, I attended a lecture in New York by a distinguished French scientist, Jacques Monod. Stunned by the clarity of his thinking, I decided on the spot that I wanted to learn more about his research into microbial genetics. The study of

16

genetics was one of the three revolutionary developments taking place in the medical sciences in the middle of the twentieth century. One involved a new understanding of viruses and how they cause disease – hence the progress with the polio vaccine. Another – my current interest at NIH – focused on the biochemical sequences that take place in all living organisms. The third was providing stunning new insights into how genes control organisms, which is the subject matter of molecular genetics.

Thinking that I might use Monod's techniques in my own experiments, I talked to Diana about the possibility of visiting France. She was excited by the prospect of a Parisian interlude, and without unreeling any red tape, the National Heart Institute agreed to provide me with a sabbatical year at the Pasteur Institute in Paris. Monod was interested in our work on enzymes, so it was no problem to arrange the visit.

We went to France in the summer of 1962, and I quickly started my second crash course in modern science, this time in microbial genetics. Monod and his colleagues at the Pasteur Institute were analyzing, in microbes, the manner in which genes trigger the responses the cells make to changes in their environments. During my stay in Paris, I learned as much from Monod, who was an unusual scientist, as I did from my lab work. Monod's sometimes heretical ideas were attracting some of the world's best scientists to his lab, and I now had a year to broaden my knowledge of the links between biochemistry and genetics.

Monod was even more brilliant than I'd thought when I first heard him speak. He had a rare ability to talk about any field in science, and I was especially impressed by his willingness to discuss seriously ideas that seemed off-the-wall. He was quick to propose explanations of important biological phenomena based on early, even minimal data. His ideas came fast, and then experimental evidence supporting his hypotheses often followed from various laboratories.

Most scientists I knew were more tightly focused and contemptuous of scientific heresy. Like Earl Stadtman, they were more constrained by their reliance on what they considered to be hard evidence. Monod, by contrast, was always willing to float an intellectual trial balloon. He had a significant influence on me: In the years that followed, I would stay open to the ideas of mavericks who were operating outside the comfortable boundaries of accepted practice. Greater risk taking had become part of my research and lifestyle. That was Monod's greatest gift to me, and I still treasure it.

\* \* \*

At the end of the year, however, we returned to the United States, to NIH, and our search for the enzymes controlling fatty acid synthesis. The science being done by Monod and his colleagues was exciting – at a world-class, Nobel Prize level – but I thought that our laboratory in Bethesda was also on the brink of a major breakthrough. We had already attracted considerable attention and were receiving applications from outstanding postdoctoral researchers. We had been joined, for instance, by Phil Majerus, a scientist of enormous intellectual capacity.

After our growing team had identified a crucial protein (ACP) and determined its composition, we were able to establish (along with several other leading scientists) that this particular substance was the central actor in a process crucial to all plants and animals – including humans. Learning that this protein is a universal component of all biological systems made this the single most exciting series of events in my scientific career.

We were doing good work in hot science, and when that happens, you receive many attractive job offers. By 1965, I had received several interesting propositions from medical schools, but each time Diana and I decided not to bite. Our "five-year plan" for NIH had been successful and gradually became a "ten-year plan," and we were settled and happy close to Washington.

Despite all our blessings, however, I was becoming restless. Medicine was not a high priority at NIH. The people who mattered were the scientists doing basic research. Isolation from medicine left me uneasy and wondering if all my training and early ideas about working with people were just evaporating. I needed to get closer to medicine again, so I was ready to listen when Washington University's School of Medicine invited me to chair its Department of Biological Chemistry. In that chair I would be following Nobel laureate Carl Cori, one of the giants of biochemistry. So Diana and I took this offer very seriously and finally decided to accept it and move to St. Louis. Now I would practice my science in a setting in which I'd be directly involved with medicine.

\* \* \*

My colleague Phil Majerus flew into orbit when he heard the news. A graduate of Washington University's School of Medicine, he proclaimed that I had just been offered the best job in the country – maybe even the world! He would be going too because he secured a primary faculty position in the Department of Internal Medicine with a joint appointment in biochemistry. Al Alberts would join us as well, even though he would be only an instructor, a humble position in an American university.

So with some sadness we left NIH and Earl Stadtman, a man who had as much impact on my career as anyone outside of my immediate family. I knew that Earl was my last true mentor and that now I would become a mentor to others. We headed into the heartland, feeling like pioneers. St. Louis and the entire Middle West was a new country for us, and I was also starting my first experience in rebuilding an organization.

To his credit, Carl Cori had left behind a department with almost no deadwood. There were only a couple of scientists whose work wasn't going anywhere. As I walked the halls and talked science with each member of the department, it was obvious whose work had momentum and whose research had plateaued. A few of my new colleagues soon realized that, as the euphemism has it, "they would be happier elsewhere." That's a harsh lesson the first time you learn it, but I have never seen a successful turnaround that did not force some people out.

Fortunately, the nucleus of my new department was solidly productive, so my job was primarily one of addition, not subtraction. We already had several outstanding biochemists – names anyone in the field would recognize – and we were able to make other outstanding appointments. Within a short time, graduate education at the medical school was blossoming. We began to get positive feedback as the word spread that Washington University Biochemistry was a "hot department."

As I became more familiar with the workings of the university, I began to explore other possibilities for creative change. We devoted substantial energy, for instance, to increasing African American participation in the medical school program. We made some mistakes along the way. But with the strong support of chancellor Bill Danforth, we were able to increase the minority representation.

Danforth's backing was also important when we set out to reorganize and bring together the university's undergraduate biology and all of its biomedical graduate programs. We consolidated them into a new Division of Biology and Biomedical Sciences. Under this new plan, we were able to raise the level of science education for the undergraduates, extend high-quality graduate work through more departments, and spread the high academic standards now established at the medical school.

Reorganization meant that faculty members had to change their routines – a transition more difficult than most people outside of the university can imagine. The merging of the faculty was tricky because the medical school was one of the best in the country, but in the 1960s several of the undergraduate and graduate programs in the biological sciences were mediocre. Our medical school hotshots looked down on most of their counterparts across the campus.

To ease the pain of creating a unified teaching organization, we had to make a good-faith showing of our new unity. At our first joint meeting to discuss the merger, some of the faculty were skeptical: "If you guys want to come over here, will you teach these undergraduate courses?" I told them I would be happy to kick off the new operation by teaching part of the introductory biochemistry course to undergrads. And I did, much to my own enjoyment.

In effect, we were able to "average up." We put pressure on the mediocre faculty in the short term and ensured that promotions and appointments would be of the highest quality in the long term. These innovations had a striking, almost immediate impact. We didn't just change the structure of the organization. What we changed were the internal values and expectations about performance as well as the external perception of what we were doing at the university. The gaps between departments began to close, in part because now all vital decisions on recruitment, promotion, and tenure were made at the Division level, where standards were very high.

This was my first major experience with reorganization as a vehicle for upgrading personnel, improving performance, and strengthening an institution's commitment to innovation. Organizations that don't change don't last. They need to be revitalized periodically if only because people tend to settle into routines and drop out of touch with their changing environments. As I now understood, one important role of a leader is to convince people, before the fact, that they should change.

\* \* \*

Although teaching and administration consumed more and more of my days, I was never far from science. Al Alberts and I were pressing ahead on several interrelated pathways. This work carried us into research involving cholesterol, a subject of substantial concern to clinicians as well as scientists in the 1970s.

Since the early 1900s, researchers had suspected a link between atherosclerosis – thickening and hardening of the arteries – and a high-fat diet. Over the years, scientists had gradually determined the structure and multiple functions of the cholesterol molecule, winning several Nobel Prizes along the way. In the 1960s, they made substantial progress in delineating cholesterol's biosynthetic pathway, that is, in determining exactly how the body makes cholesterol.

Meanwhile, interesting epidemiological findings had tightened the link between cholesterol and coronary heart disease, the cause of heart attacks. Now my goal of taking my science back to people appeared to be almost within reach. I had moved further and further away from bench science. I still directed the experiments, but I no longer performed them. All of my lab work was now being done by the hands of others: a growing team of energetic, very smart postdoctoral scientists; a few graduate students; some dedicated, skillful technicians; and of course Al Alberts.

By the mid-1970s, our research efforts had carried us rather far into the analysis of the form and function of lipids, including cholesterol. Studying enzymes, I concluded, was the best way to understand normal cell functions as well as disease states in all animals, including humans. My early interest in cardiology made the role of cholesterol in heart disease particularly intriguing for me as did the potential to find enzyme inhibitors that might actually alter disease states.

\* \* \*

I was thinking along these lines when I received an invitation to consult with Merck & Co., Inc., in Rahway, almost next door to the luncheonette where I had worked. As a physician and scientist, I had had very little to do with the pharmaceutical industry or its sales representatives. But I was willing to return to Merck's laboratories to help their scientists better understand what was going on at the cutting edge of biochemistry and enzymology. A Merck vice president of research, David Jacobus, invited me to consult at their laboratories, and I quickly discovered I had plenty to tell them.

Merck had a long record of superb accomplishments in organic and fermentation chemistry. Organic synthesis had yielded important vitamins, and the Merck Research Laboratories had also made important contributions to the development of penicillin and streptomycin, the first effective treatment for tuberculosis.[1] But by the

---

[1] The name at that time was the Merck Sharp & Dohme Research Laboratories, but to prevent confusion we have throughout used its present name, Merck Research Laboratories.

mid-1970s, organic chemistry was no longer providing adequate targets for drug discovery. Perhaps, I thought, biochemistry could help.

When I visited Rahway, it was apparent that the company's laboratories had fallen behind the leading edge of my field. I gave as much advice as I could, but I came away with the strong impression that their scientists were not really prepared to listen to an outsider. I was disappointed with this reception, but I became more interested in Merck when they invited me back the next year.

CHAPTER THREE

# Turn Around

MY SECOND EXPERIENCE TURNING AROUND AN ORGANI-
zation was a substantially more difficult job in a setting
that was new to me. Many of the ideas and values that I had accumulated over the years were useful, but when Merck & Co., Inc.,
offered me a job in November 1974, I knew very little about the
pharmaceutical business and virtually nothing about the American business system. I certainly didn't know whether I could lead
Merck Research Laboratories (MRL) to a medicine that would
cure or prevent a disease.

But I was convinced that, if the company improved the quality
of its research and MRL's strategy for drug discovery, it would
have a much better chance of someday developing new therapies
that would really make a difference. That was the hook for me –
believing I could have a positive impact on the company's ability
to reach that laudable goal. After our customary, extended family
discussion, Diana and I agreed that we should accept this new
offer, frame a new ten-year plan, and move our growing family
(now including Andrew and Ellen) back East to New Jersey.

The truth is that when we decided to accept the company's offer, I didn't know everything Merck was doing. The company had twenty-six plants in the United States and thirty-nine overseas. Over 26,000 employees were developing, producing, and distributing prescription drugs, specialty chemicals, and animal health and environmental products. I knew nothing about subsidiaries like the Calgon Corporation and the Baltimore Aircoil Company. Instead, I was armed with an impressionistic blend of Rahway memories, family lore, and recent personal encounters. My consulting visits had given me a very clear view of what was going on in only one part of the firm, the research laboratories.

There, I could see that Merck had responded to the changes taking place in the medical sciences by hiring several biochemists. But the new people seemed to have had little impact on the basic strategy of drug discovery in the laboratories. The organic chemists were still kings of the hill at Merck. One program they were optimistic about involved halofenate, a product candidate that lowered cholesterol.[1] It had advanced to clinical testing in patients even though they didn't know the mechanism of action at the molecular level. They didn't know which enzymes, if any, the compound inhibited. That worried me.

Historically, most drugs had been discovered the way Merck found halofenate. The process of discovery was empirical, whether it was conducted in a laboratory or by simple folk observation of what happened when people ingested something. This is how aspirin, morphine, digitalis, and vitamin C came into use. The empirical process works, but it depends on luck and takes an enormous amount of time to bear results.

---

[1] Throughout, our reference is to "blood cholesterol," that is, the level of serum cholesterol.

Starting around the 1940s, scientists had sped up the discovery process by testing drugs on animals. They produced "animal models" of human disease, usually in a mouse or rat, and then treated the animal with various chemicals to see which was the most effective.[2] The most promising chemicals were then refined or modified to increase potency and reduce side effects and were subsequently tested on humans.

Merck and the rest of the pharmaceutical industry were also discovering drugs by doing large numbers of blind screening experiments using cell cultures. Merck's researchers were either treating these cultures with broths isolated from soil microorganisms from different parts of the world or with chemicals drawn from the chemical "library" company scientists had built up over the years. The library consisted of compounds that had demonstrated pharmacological activity in an animal or cell culture screen. An active chemical constituted a "lead." It was then the job of Merck chemists to tinker methodically with the molecule's atoms to eliminate undesirable properties that might cause side effects.

This classical pharmaceutical industry method was based on synthetic organic chemistry and pharmacology. Using animals, a researcher could run perhaps twelve experiments a day. Using cell cultures, he or she could run 100 in a single day. Importantly, both in experiments with cell cultures and in animal research, the process was random and slow because there was no understanding of the actual chemical targets at the molecular level.

I believed that targeting specific enzymes offered a much more efficient method for developing drugs. All enzymes have active

---

[2] Don't let the expression "animal models" confuse you. It just means they were using animals.

sites, and biochemists use the metaphor of a lock and key to describe the start of the chemical transformation that takes place in these sites. The substance to be acted upon (the key) must fit the active site (the lock) exactly or nothing happens. When a chemical interferes with the precise fit, the interaction doesn't take place, and a whole chain of sequential steps is interrupted. This sequence could be one that produced cholesterol or it could be a disease process such as an infection. By isolating and understanding the structure of a crucial enzyme, researchers could greatly increase the odds of discovering a chemical agent that would block the reaction and stop the sequence.

Because I was already dedicated to this targeted approach, I wasn't excited about halofenate. The compound didn't seem to inhibit any of the specific enzymes in the control of cholesterol synthesis. Worse, as the clinical trials progressed, the company's researchers found that in addition to lowering cholesterol, halofenate also lowered triglycerides and blood sugar. Some of the researchers were delighted with so many potentially beneficial effects. But I was stunned that they were continuing with a product candidate that did so many things. As the multiple effects indicated, they didn't fully understand exactly what the drug was doing at the molecular level. As a physician, I wanted them to provide very specific drugs for specific conditions that were fully understood. Even though I had no practical experience in drug discovery, I knew there had to be a better way to do things.

That's what I had told CEO Henry Gadsden, when Merck started to recruit me. On one of my visits, I said to him, "If I become head of the laboratories, I'll want to make dramatic changes in the way they try to find new drugs." Gadsden replied, "If we didn't want big changes, we wouldn't be talking to you."

So I knew what I had to do when I decided to enter the corporate world. The laboratories needed a great deal of organizational repair work. The business was in good shape, paying regular dividends and continuing to increase its sales. The problems that concerned me were below that level of the firm and were internal to the Merck Research Laboratories.

There, I knew I had lots of walking and talking to do. I understood that introducing changes in this kind of well-established scientific organization would take a long time. I started by carefully studying the internal memos and then scheduling a review of every research group at Merck. At each meeting I stayed as long as necessary – at least half a day and often more – to understand each project. It was a very intense study.

MRL was a large operation, much larger than anything I had worked with at the university. That year's budget was $125 million, and there were 1,800 people in research and development. Many of the researchers were in Rahway, but there was also a large laboratory complex in West Point, Pennsylvania.

I quickly discovered that Rahway and West Point were two very different worlds. The Pennsylvania organization had belonged to Sharp & Dohme (S&D), a pharmaceutical company acquired by Merck in 1953 for its marketing and sales capability. According to the original plan, Merck was to supply the research power and S&D the promotional know-how and distribution network, thus blending the two pharmaceutical organizations into one seamless, integrated operation.

But twenty-two years later, the employees at West Point still said, "I work for Sharp & Dohme." They called Merck's Rahway headquarters the "Emerald City" and refused to identify with Merck even though the CEO, Henry Gadsden, had come up through the West Point organization. The following president, John Horan, had worked in both Rahway and West Point, but he was no more successful than Gadsden in dissolving the powerful sense of separateness that persisted at West Point.

The people in both organizations took great pride in what they were doing: Rahway was known for its research and chemical manufacturing. West Point, though it also housed a large research group, was best known for its manufacturing of tablets, capsules, and injectables, its marketing, and its sales to physicians.

Neither group would accept the complementary nature of this very successful merger, and the tension between the two organizations made my job more difficult. I was the new research boss on the block, driving down from the Emerald City to tell the West Point pros how to improve the way they did their research.

Aside from Dr. Maurice R. Hilleman, who had successfully developed some of the country's most important pediatric vaccines, the scientists at West Point were using the same traditional research strategy as those at Rahway. Repeated failures didn't persuade them to change this technique: Years of random screening had hardened them to expect failure with most "leads." From time to time there were successes, which made them unwilling to change a strategy that seemed as logical to them as it was illogical to me. I returned to Rahway pondering my options and looking for a new way to turn the operation around.

I had to convince them to target a particular enzyme involved in a disease process and identify a medicine to react directly with that molecule. Once we identified our target enzyme, the medicinal chemists could design inhibitors in the laboratory, and the microbiologists and natural product chemists could look for inhibitors in nature. The search process would, I posited, be much faster since experiments would not involve animals or cells in the initial phase. Hundreds of experiments could be done each day. If we could find inhibitors that fitted tightly into the active site of the target enzyme and nowhere else, our drugs would also be likely to have fewer side effects.

This approach, which relies on better scientific understanding, had already been used sporadically in the industry. Beta-blocker drugs for treating high blood pressure were discovered by targeting specific receptor molecules. But no laboratory had adopted the new strategy as its primary mode of discovery, and when we started the transformation of MRL most of the industry was still almost exclusively using screening in animal models of disease or cell cultures.

When I set out to turn the labs toward the new strategy, I was not about to fire all the scientists at West Point or Rahway who were skeptical about my style of targeted research. I respected what Merck had accomplished using traditional techniques of discovery. So I erred on the side of tolerance and patience. Besides coaxing and guiding, I wanted to prove by example that biochemical targeting was the best route to drug discovery.

In this, I was once again indebted to Al Alberts, who decided to give up tenure at Washington University and help me move our laboratory to Rahway. A number of our postdoctoral fellows also came along, giving us a core group familiar with the latest developments in lipid biosynthesis.

As I waded into my new job at Merck, I quickly discovered that the powerful sense of unity and comradeship that had existed at Washington University didn't exist in a pharmaceutical firm. Relationships in the business were cordial but more formal – especially if you moved across divisional lines. The people in the research division were just as dedicated to science as were their counterparts at the university. But the Merck researchers had very little in common with the people in the marketing and sales divisions or the central administration. Although these groups were all friendly, their differences in training and interests kept them apart. Each acknowledged the importance of all of the other groups, but most of them understood only their own challenges. We all ate lunch in the same cafeteria, but the research people ate early and were leaving by the time the corporate types came in.

All of these intricacies of corporate life were new to me, as I struggled to climb the steep part of my pharmaceutical learning curve. One of the first things I discovered as I reviewed the research projects was that most of the groups were trying to do too much, not too little. Instead of concentrating on one or two promising projects, they were conducting research on eight or nine. They were seldom pleased about narrowing the focus of their work. When I tried to get the endocrinologists to focus all their resources on their most promising lines of research, for instance, the head of that laboratory promptly left and joined the Yale Medical School faculty.

My transition from academic to corporate life involved an introduction to "Management by Objectives" (MBO), a program used by many American corporations. When I started with the company, I had never heard of MBO or any other technique for managing personnel. Since I had never "reported" to anyone in my career, I at first found the entire procedure crazy. As I learned, each employee at Merck sat down periodically with a supervisor, the person to whom he or she "reported," to discuss goals for the coming year. The pair also regularly reviewed the employee's progress in achieving the previous year's goals.

Merck had been using MBO for two decades and wasn't about to change the plan, so I decided to take it seriously. I could see that most employees were simply reproducing their job descriptions, listing everything they were going to do during the next year. That could generate as many as twenty-five objectives. At the end of the year, they'd go over the list again, highlight what had been successful, and explain that someone else's shortcomings had prevented them from accomplishing the remainder.

I decided to change that procedure. I announced that at MRL we would each have a maximum of five goals. At first they went bananas. But they calmed down after they'd actually tried the new procedure. We were always able to agree on their top five priorities, and by doing that people reporting to me set goals that they and I agreed were critical to the success of MRL – goals that were challenging but, in my estimation, achievable. I made a point of frequently discussing the goals with our research people, making suggestions I thought would help them.

In my way of running MRL, their goals were my goals. They quickly understood my way of working out the strategy in research. They recognized that we were in it together and appreciated that I was determined not to allow us to fail.

My focus was on people, not structure. I was interested in changing the way we did things, but I didn't believe – and still don't believe today – that you can turn a business around just by changing the way it's organized. The key to making your operation more effective and innovative is to recruit and encourage talented risk takers – the more the better. When I became president of the laboratories in 1976, I quickly set out to recruit more of these entrepreneurial types for MRL. I began to look over the files of all of our job candidates and to interview every senior scientist and physician who was going to be offered a position in Rahway or West Point.

Wherever our operation was weak, I was particularly attentive to the new hires. I thought, for instance, that neither our clinical research nor our engineering was as good as it should have been.

I was just as much an elitist at Merck as I had been at Washington University. When I saw a second-rate résumé, I just said no. The key thing I looked at was performance in previous positions – either in training at a university or in a job. Had the applicant taken difficult courses? Carried a heavy course load? Was he or she involved in sports or in other extracurricular activities? Had he or she been a leader? What had been accomplished in previous positions?

We were seeking outstanding people, and they are recognizable. Some department heads shy away from recruiting outstanding people because of fear they will not fit in well, will be too ambitious, or will become dissatisfied in the job and leave to move up in the organization. Those were the people I wanted to recruit, tigers anxious to show us all how to do it better. But that was not a popular position when I first went to Merck. In due time, the company changed. As department heads recognized what could be accomplished by outstanding new recruits, they shed their inhibitions and began to look for their own tigers.

In the case of clinical research, I rejected about a dozen candidates in a row, and finally the head of the operation came to see me. "Why are you turning down all of these good people?" he asked. I explained what I wanted to accomplish. Exasperated, he finally blurted out, "You wouldn't have hired me!" I just looked at him without saying anything because we both knew he was right.

Gradually, we began to upgrade our recruitment across the board. It couldn't be done quickly. You had to bring in top-grade people who were good learners and incrementally improve the operation. I asked everyone in charge of a department or research group to list the top eight or ten schools in their field. Then, I told them I wanted to see applicants mostly from those schools. They groaned. "This is snobbish," some complained. Others were more upset. "My God!" they said, "I didn't graduate from one of those schools! What does that say about me?" But I told them, "You picked the best schools in your field, not me. We're just trying to be efficient." I said, "I can't see why we would recruit elsewhere. Of course there can be terrific people at any school, but let's play the odds."

The truth was that most department heads had been recruiting at the schools from which *they* had graduated. That was okay in some cases, but if their alma maters were weak, the weaknesses in our program were being reinforced.

\* \* \*

If recruitment had not been absolutely vital to the company, I wouldn't have devoted this much attention to it. Recruitment for R&D had long been an uphill battle for pharmaceutical firms because the academic training grounds for scientists were oriented to basic, not applied, research. During the post-World War expansion of government funding for science at universities, many academic scientists had begun to believe that what they did was the only thing to do.

Fortunately for my efforts at Merck, applied research became more fashionable as university growth leveled off and government funds for basic research got tighter. That transition, taking place in the late 1970s, began to have a decisive impact on our recruitment efforts. Meanwhile, I discouraged our research department heads from hiring people from other companies unless we were starting work in an entirely new area of science or engineering. Then we needed a seasoned research person with industry experience in that field. But hiring from other pharmaceutical companies just seemed to be a way for headhunters to make money and to provide the lucky applicant with a raise he or she wouldn't otherwise have been given on the basis of performance. I wanted to build strength from within, gradually improving the organization until ideally we could promote most of our talented senior people out of our own ranks.

I was also able to improve MRL by recognizing the talents of the people who were already there. A good example was Dr. Arthur Patchett, who had joined MRL shortly after receiving his Ph.D. from Harvard and completing a postdoctoral fellowship at NIH. On the basis of his outstanding research talents, he'd quickly become head of the entire synthetic chemistry operation at Rahway. He was a brilliant chemist, but he was also very young. Not yet a great manager, he flopped and was banished to a dungeon-like laboratory building out of the mainstream. His boss had him making random peptides, removing the solvent from the reaction mixture, and then running portions of it through assays to see if it showed any signs of activity. He'd been doing this for a couple of years when I arrived at Merck.

I could see that Art was an unusually talented scientist, and I thought he was probably the kind of risk taker willing to tackle really difficult projects. He was too talented to be cranking out random assortments of peptides. I said: "Art, this can't be the way to discover drugs. It's not going to work. Wouldn't you like to target an enzyme molecule and try to make a drug that way?" He was, of course, ready for a change. Once we decided on a new project that he wanted to pursue, he became an unusually creative scientist. Art was one of the most innovative chemists in MRL, but he had to be allowed to be productive.

A rescue of a different sort took place in regulatory affairs, the department responsible for Merck's applications for FDA approval of its new drugs and vaccines. For all pharmaceutical companies, getting FDA approval is a complex, expensive, time-consuming, and life-or-death matter. If you become very good at it, you can actually use this capability as a bargaining chip in dealing with other firms in the industry. If you're not good at it, your company will lose a great deal of money, or maybe go under.

This is how it works. When a researcher discovers a novel substance that looks promising, the company files for a patent, which gives it exclusive marketing rights for a period of years. The company at that time then invested an average of about $800 million to develop a new drug from this substance (this figure has gone way up since the 1990s). The new medicine can be brought to market only after large-scale clinical studies demonstrate that it is safe and effective in humans, and the study results are then compiled by the research group and submitted to the FDA for approval.

By the time a medicine received FDA approval, on average about eight years of the patent have been used up – leaving about twelve years for sales of the patent-protected product. The faster the FDA grants approval, the faster the product can be launched and the sales begun. Any time lost because of delays in regulatory approval causes a loss of sales revenues during the patent-protected life of the product.

Every pharmaceutical company wants as perfect a regulatory filing as possible by the research group. Incomplete or ambiguous data will cause the FDA to request additional explanations or even additional experiments. Time and sales will be lost. Even worse, the FDA can decide the results are not convincing and turn down the application.

I learned that our head of regulatory affairs had long considered himself a glorified mailman. When I asked him, "What's your job?," he said, "I file the New Drug Application." I pressed harder: "What does that mean to you?" He replied, "I gather the information, put it in a book, and send it to the FDA." He was in effect orchestrating the applications without becoming engaged with the data being presented to the government.

One of our compounds – *Timoptic*, a beta-blocker to treat glaucoma – had produced some unexpected results in one of the studies in animals. Although one interpretation was that the drug could be dangerous in humans, a series of ingenious experiments demonstrated that the drug was safe, clearing the way for FDA approval. When discussing *Timoptic* with the head of regulatory affairs, I found he didn't understand the experiments exonerating the beta-blocker and planned to ask our technical experts to explain the results to the FDA. I told him that the head of regulatory affairs is responsible for FDA strategy and that he and his colleagues must understand all of the data presented for approval well enough to explain them to the agency.

He was a very bright man who understood at once that he and his group were now expected to do a different job and that he would need a better class of professionals – scientists at least as good as those in clinical research – to get that job done. He began recruiting aggressively and found some good scientists willing to give up lab work, especially those not currently working on an exciting project. By enlisting people with better scientific training, he began to turn the regulatory affairs operation around, and instead of running away from the challenge, he became one of the architects of the new order.

\* \* \*

Much of my time was spent talking to researchers about their work or listening to formal presentations about their projects. In the pharmaceutical industry, a researcher can easily spend ten to fifteen years on a project before it produces an approved drug.

I had no problem with such long-range projects if they looked promising. The ones that worried me were those taking three to five years without producing a glimmer of success.

I tried to eliminate those projects in two ways. One was to keep talking and listening on a one-to-one basis with the scientists. My private conversations were far more useful than any of the regularly scheduled, formal show-and-tell presentations made to senior members of research management. It would greatly embarrass a presenter in front of the entire organization to point out, say, that the experimental results were insufficient to support a conclusion or that the proposed future experiments were not appropriate, given what was already known. As a result, comments were hedged at these meetings.

In general, I found that large public meetings of almost any sort were fine for disseminating information but very inefficient, even counterproductive, for making critical evaluations or decisions on strategic directions. When I talked science face-to-face, I got a more accurate picture of what was or wasn't working at the bench level of research. Often I heard the most important things while standing in the lunch line with the scientists, walking to a lecture, or waiting out in the hall before a presentation.

The scientists leveled with me because I was a scientist myself and I understood their difficulties. They knew that, as head of the lab, I took on each project as my own, suggesting solutions to help them solve their problems. Some project leaders were reluctant to change because so much time had already been invested in the current effort. Some were unwilling to admit that an approach wasn't going to work. So they procrastinated for months or years. I wanted definite objectives with a defined time and effort. If the goals could not be achieved, then I wanted to try something that was more likely to work.

Mainly, I let them know that I was invested in every step of the process. There's no substitute for that kind of involvement if you want a high-morale, high-intensity research organization. The best way to get a researcher to stop a bad project is to convince him or her to work on something much more exciting with the prospect of making an important contribution.

My second elimination tactic was to press all of the groups to prioritize their projects continually and shift resources toward the most promising areas of research. It worked much as it had with MBO. "Look," I'd say, "if you're going to make this kind of inhibitor this year, you'll never do it with only four chemists. So let's put ten chemists on that project." Often the reply I got was, "Aaach! Where are they going to come from?" Then I'd point out that they had chemists working on projects with very little prospect of succeeding for many years, if ever. "Yeah," they would say, "but these good old guys have been working on that for many years." We had to break through the "good old guy" barrier.

In the late 1970s we finally began to make considerable progress in Merck's laboratories by keeping the pressure on across the whole spectrum of research activities: establishing new hypotheses, setting up new screens, judging productivity of older screens, identifying product leads, identifying product candidates, interpreting results of clinical studies, and updating the patenting to ensure exclusivity in product ownership. We used our annual research conferences at Seaview, a resort on the southern New Jersey coast just north of Atlantic City, to develop a strategic plan that would keep the pressure on across all these fronts.

At Seaview, all the project directors gave presentations on what their research teams had accomplished and what they expected in the year ahead. We discussed drug candidates evolving from our own research, possible product breakthroughs outside of Merck, and the possibility of Merck research entering a new field based on activities in other pharmaceutical or academic laboratories. If Merck research was not working in a particular field, could we license a product candidate from another source? Discussions also covered the potential costs of our new product candidates as projected by our research chemical engineers and finance people.

An annual strategic plan would ultimately evolve in which the costs of all the activities would be tallied. In addition to the annual review of strategy, some time was also given to an update on our five-year strategy. This was especially important because we needed to project the impact of future clinical studies, usually the most expensive stage of product development.

The MRL leaders decided which projects would continue and which would be killed. It was uncanny how much exciting information was generated just a few months before this meeting, and the new findings seemed always to make it more difficult to stop a project. Because it is very tough for project leaders to pull the plug on the losers, the Seaview sessions focused on sifting and analyzing all the information that would enable us to decide whether it would be "thumbs up" or "thumbs down" for each of the projects.

When research had produced viable candidates, we pumped in enormous resources to develop the product. When projects had established proof of principle, that is, demonstrating that the product of their research had the desired effect and would work against human disease, we provided the support they needed to optimize a lead before selecting a product candidate. We also tried to identify projects in which the team had a promising hypothesis but had not yet been able to achieve proof of principle. Then, too, we sifted out proposals for new undertakings based on hypotheses generated by our scientists from their own research or results from either university or competing industrial laboratories.

These sessions were long and tough. We spent most of our time on the long-term projects for which proof of principle had not been achieved, with everyone straining to devise an experiment that would either lead to a product candidate or kill the project. There were winners and losers every year.

\* \* \*

Over the years, one of my special delights was to watch new scientific leaders emerge at the Seaview meetings. Leaders in science are easy to identify: They're risk takers who are the most productive scientists and who come up with more new ideas, new experiments to test hypotheses, and new and exciting results in their projects. They attract new recruits because their projects generate scientific excitement. Risk taking is an important aspect of scientific progress. The best scientists are willing, on the basis of a unique understanding of available data, to move their research into important new areas in which there are few precedents and therefore a higher probability of failure. Despite the risk, industry depends on these special people for breakthrough products, and I knew they were the key to the future of MRL and Merck.

While we were making progress at MRL, I was acutely aware of the mistakes I was making as I tried to transform this large, proud organization. Determined to produce a research turnaround, I pushed too hard on the recruitment process early on. When I encountered resistance from outstanding candidates suspicious of "applied research," I gave too much away. I began to promise some of them that they could continue with their own projects, just moving them from the university to MRL. Certain that they would shortly get caught up in the excitement of drug discovery, I thought we could gradually refocus their research if it turned out not to have any practical implications.

I was wrong. Some of them happily toiled away at their own basic research, paying no attention to what was happening around them. So much for infectious excitement. When I tried to get them to take part in any of our leading projects, they reminded me of the promise I had made. I keep my promises, so I was left with a small group of extremely talented people doing hot science that was more likely to help their publication records over the next twenty years than it was to help Merck. I stopped making that promise and began to be explicit about what we were doing and what I expected at MRL.

We employed many outstanding scientists who regularly published their research results, but we didn't pretend to be a university. Merck Research Laboratory's goal was to be the best laboratory in the world for drug discovery. After recovering from my initial mistakes, I tried to keep that objective fixed clearly in the minds of our new scientific personnel – especially when they were being recruited.

I was also too slow in dealing with the "backup problem." When I arrived at MRL, I didn't even realize there *was* such a problem. My background in university and NIH research hadn't prepared me for this one. But what I began to see as I settled into my new job was that once basic research produced a promising compound, the team stopped working on the entire project while their candidate went through safety assessment and moved into clinical studies. The scientists who had discovered the molecule would normally be holding their breath, fearful their candidate would fail the tests. After all, many have worked in pharmaceutical research their entire career and never developed a successful drug. Failures are far more numerous than successes.

But I wasn't worried about their state of mind. I wanted them to be preparing MRL for two possibilities. If the first compound was toxic or otherwise unsuccessful, they should already have in the wings a second, related backup candidate different enough in structure that it might lack the problem we had uncovered. If the first compound succeeded, they should be working on the improved follow-up drug – one with greater potency, one with fewer side effects, or one that could be given fewer times a day.

To deal with this situation, we established a new rule. We never stopped work on a discovery project until the candidate cleared the proof of concept clinical studies. To pass the proof of concept, the drug candidate had to demonstrate its beneficial effect in initial limited human clinical studies. This kept the people in basic and clinical research talking to one another. It also provided us with some outstanding follow-up drugs in the cardiovascular field. The rule worked, but I should have moved in that direction faster and more forcefully. I was learning, but it was an expensive, on-the-job education.

My biggest mistake resulted from my unwillingness to push harder at West Point. I had made some inroads there, but resistance to my research strategy was deep and strong. The leaders there, distinguished scientists who were experts in their disciplines, were not accepting the molecular targeting approach. They were convinced the traditional methodology would continue to generate product candidates and were entirely certain of their future success. I let them continue in their way for many months. Looking back, I can see in precise dollar terms what that cost our company.

At that time, the West Point researchers were working on a potential treatment for peptic ulcers. It was a compound able to suppress the secretion of acid in the stomach of animals. I quickly realized that they didn't know *how* it worked. I tried to coax them into figuring out just what their compound did at the molecular level. When problems developed in the safety tests, they tried to solve them by tinkering with the molecule. Meanwhile, Merck was losing ground in the race to develop new therapies.

I was worried because the field of ulcer treatments was experiencing a decisive breakthrough in the 1970s. At a SmithKline laboratory in England, James Black developed a molecule that suppressed the secretion of acid by blocking a specific receptor molecule in the stomach, precisely what I wanted our Merck scientists to do. Since peptic ulcers had been treated with acid neutralizers (antiacids) for many years, stopping the secretion of acid in the stomach made enormous sense. This was just the kind of molecular targeting I wanted MRL to conduct. In Black's case, the result was *Tagamet*, a breakthrough treatment for peptic ulcers.

On one of my trips to West Point, I discussed what Black was doing. I'd already made this speech several times, but this time I was certain the new evidence about Black's accomplishments would enable us to turn the corner – at last. But it didn't. The Merck researchers circled the wagons around their project. They believed they were on the verge of identifying a potent, safe compound that reduced acid secretion in dog stomachs. They felt they had a winner even though they didn't understand how it worked.

I wasn't one to bludgeon people, but I didn't give up. I talked to them every time I visited, which was once or twice a week. Each time I was there, they showed me new data, new curves on the graph demonstrating improvements to their compound. I grew increasingly nervous as the months dragged past and SmithKline was getting closer to market.

At last my colleagues decided they had optimized their compound, and they then sent it into safety assessment in animals. It turned out to be grossly toxic. I wasn't surprised, because they didn't know the compound's mechanism of action. I knew it could be reacting with several molecules other than those targeted by Jim Black, and I was surprised that some of the senior scientists involved didn't seem to learn much from the experience.

But because I wasn't persuasive enough, or wasn't tough enough, or perhaps because I was uncertain of myself in this new setting, Merck lost several years of lead time in peptic ulcers. We finally ignored the advice of our own research team and licensed a compound from another company that was given the trade name *Pepcid*. In its prescription and over-the-counter formulations, *Pepcid* became a billion-dollar-a-year product.

I took some consolation from the fact that *Pepcid* was the first product Merck had ever licensed from an outside source. For years the laboratory had resisted licensing, largely because of an n-i-h (not-invented-here) mentality. Only MRL discoveries, the scientists maintained, were good enough for Merck. *Pepcid* blasted that myth, setting the stage for later transactions that were critical to the company's future.

But consolation prizes seldom console, and this one didn't leave me happy with my own performance. Had we shifted our approach earlier, we might have discovered our own compound and avoided paying royalties for a licensed product. Add that to the roughly three years of revenue we lost, and it should be clear why I put this experience on the liability side of my personal ledger.

One reason I was hesitant to knock heads over research strategies was the stunning success achieved with ivermectin – the drug I described in the first pages of this book. This amazing antiparasitic drug was discovered shortly after I arrived in Rahway, and it was discovered in the old style. A product of random screenings of natural microbial broths (using a unique animal model of a gastrointestinal parasitic disease), it became the leading animal health product of the 1980s and 1990s. Ivermectin kills parasitic worms in the gastrointestinal tracts of horses, cattle, sheep, and pigs. It also kills biting flies.

Around the world, wherever animals accumulate parasites, one of the several formulations of ivermectin has long been the overwhelming drug of choice. In countries like Australia and New Zealand, which have more livestock than people, the impact of ivermectin on productivity is extremely significant to their economies. This product also kills dog heartworms. If you have a dog that you treat once a month to prevent heartworms, that drug is probably ivermectin.

Reflecting on ivermectin, I reached two conclusions. First, I saw that the traditional techniques could still produce important products. Second, in the transition to molecular targeting, we would continue to use random searches where we might have an advantage through uniqueness. I thus favored scientists who developed animal model screens that were particular to MRL and that used unique sources of new compounds. I remained open to using more than one strategy of drug research, and I continued to be tolerant of scientists who could convince me they were on the edge of a significant discovery. In those cases there was always the possibility that a few more months would actually make a big difference.

\* \* \*

What grade did I give myself as a leader in pharmaceutical innovation? In the first few years, I would give myself a B. I had made some progress, but I had not yet turned MRL around. I had made some mistakes along the way. By grinding against the grain of the established practices in drug discovery, I was winning some converts to targeted molecular research. But I would not be able

47

to bring off a wholesale conversion until my strategy produced a blockbuster drug. I knew that. I also knew that the most likely candidate for success was the program in cardiovascular disease, my own area of specialization. We had to show that MRL could convert basic knowledge about biosynthesis into new drugs for people suffering from hypertension or the effects of high cholesterol.

# CHAPTER FOUR

# New Drugs and Public Safety

S INCE THE REAL TEST OF MY LEADERSHIP IN RESEARCH
was the program in cardiovascular disease, Al Alberts, Art
Patchett, and their research teams were on center stage at MRL.
Patchett was working on hypertension and Alberts was trying to
discover a drug that would safely lower cholesterol levels.[1] Both
teams were using the new strategy of drug discovery, so I had a big
investment in their research, as did the millions of people suffering
from heart disease.

After Al and I had reviewed the literature on cholesterol
research, we had quickly decided that he and his coworkers should
target the rate-limiting enzyme in the biosynthesis of cholesterol.[2]
It was less clear how to proceed from that point, but we sought
leads from two sources. One was the library of compounds that

---

[1]  As before, all of our references to cholesterol refer to the serum cholesterol produced internally, not to the cholesterol resulting from a person's diet.
[2]  This was HMG-CoA reductase.

Merck chemists had developed over many years and could tap for this specific purpose. The other was nature.

On the nature path, we were able to get help from Art Patchett and our microbiologists who could employ a technology they had devised to screen soil microorganisms from various parts of the world. They isolated the microorganisms and grew them in small cultures in the laboratory and then in larger fermentation broths. The resulting broth was extracted to separate any interesting microbial products for testing. These cultures were a potential source of the molecule Al Alberts needed.

Merck Research Laboratories also had a deep and talented group of chemists, and the competition between the microbiologists and the chemists became intense. The chemists, who had long been the kings of research at MRL, were certain they would come up with a winner. They put significant resources into the search for a compound to inhibit our vital enzyme.

The microbiologists were also proud of what they had achieved in past years. During the Second World War, Merck had made important contributions to the process of mass-producing penicillin, and, after the war, the company's microbiologists had played a leading role in the discovery and development of streptomycin, the first effective treatment for tuberculosis.

I was an advocate of fermentation broths so long as we targeted a specific molecule. My mentor Earl Stadtman had been trained originally in soil microbiology, and I had inherited his respect for nature's ability to develop ingenious new substances of potential interest to man. So we had reason to believe that a screen of soil microorganisms designed to search for an inhibitor of the rate-limiting enzyme in cholesterol synthesis might be successful.

Al Alberts presided as the chemists raced down one path and the microbiologists down another. Al and I had a hunch that microbiology might cross the finish line first. We knew that Akira Endo, a scientist at the Japanese pharmaceutical firm Sankyo, had already reported on a compound called "compactin" that inhibited our crucial enzyme. According to the reports, Sankyo's product was a potent natural substance that could be taken orally. We were encouraged by this news but nervous, of course, because Merck was in a competitive race.

Fortunately, Al was still working long hours and was unable to stay away from his laboratory when he was awaiting results from an experiment. Art Patchett provided the microbial extracts produced by his team, and then Al and his colleague Julie Chen tested these substances in a high-throughput enzyme screen they had developed for this project. Using this technology, they were able to test large numbers of molecules quickly. Nervous about Sankyo, we nevertheless settled down for what we were certain would be a long search process.

Suddenly, however, Al found what we wanted. It was unbelievable. But the assays in 1978 clearly indicated that *Aspergillus terreus*, a common soil microorganism found around the world, was producing something that was active against our target enzyme. Al and Julie Chen were stunned when they got positive results so quickly. But then they had to wait until the chemists isolated the active substance and determined its structure. When they finished their research, we would know whether we had just rediscovered Sankyo's compactin. We hadn't. Although related structurally to compactin, our molecule, lovastatin, was a unique new compound.

We quickly put MRL on red alert and concentrated all the resources Al could effectively use on this single compound. In a research organization the size of MRL, that's a large number of people with many different talents. In addition to the chemists and microbiologists, the team now included chemical engineers, spectroscopists, pharmacologists, and toxicologists. The microbiologists determined the optimal conditions for growing the microorganism. The chemical engineers isolated the lovastatin in large quantities. Spectroscopists determined its chemical structure. Pharmacologists studied its effects in live animals, and the toxicologists studied lovastatin to demonstrate any possible harmful effects by feeding it to mice, rats, and rabbits. We also started to assemble a clinical research team and prepped marketing.

Initially, neither clinical research nor marketing got excited. They had been burned by their experience with halofenate. Besides, to them, the "cholesterol hypothesis" was still just a hypothesis. They were willing to get started, but they wanted to see more evidence that lowering cholesterol levels was good for you. They doubted that lovastatin would be any safer or more effective than halofenate and other older drugs – none of which were very effective.

Al and I, on the other hand, believed in lovastatin because it targeted a specific enzyme in the cholesterol pathway. It would, we thought, be safer and more effective than any drug previously available. We never questioned for a moment the epidemiological and other evidence supporting the "cholesterol hypothesis." We were convinced that cholesterol – and in particular low-density lipoprotein cholesterol, LDL – caused the buildup of plaque in coronary arteries and heart disease.

We were like a small army, intense and aggressive, focusing all our forces on a breakthrough in the enemy's lines. Al Alberts was the general in charge, and I was the chief of staff, making certain he had access to every researcher and piece of equipment he needed. As the pace picked up, the excitement steadily mounted, and the competition with Sankyo heightened the thrill of discovery.

During 1978 and 1979, MRL carried out hundreds of experiments to improve our understanding of what exactly lovastatin did to the targeted enzyme. When we studied the effects it had in animals, the tests indicated that it caused a dramatic reduction in cholesterol levels. Many of the earliest experiments were done in rats and mice, but when we experimented with dogs, they responded more readily with greater cholesterol reduction at lower doses. Meanwhile, we were preparing large amounts of the drug in the pilot plant so that the toxicology experiments could be completed, opening the way for initial studies in humans. All of this was moving at a whirlwind pace.

I had an emotional commitment that went far beyond science and drug discovery. Al Alberts and I had started on the trail to lovastatin in the 1950s when we began to work together on lipid biosynthesis at NIH. Now, almost a quarter of a century later, we were still together and on the verge of turning microbial biochemistry and enzyme targeting into a major factor in the treatment of human disease. Success with lovastatin would, I thought, create a consensus at MRL in favor of targeted molecular research.

That outcome was all the more likely because Art Patchett and his colleagues were in fast forward during these same months with a new enzyme inhibitor that reduced high blood pressure. There were still doubters in the laboratories, but with these two promising drug candidates on fast tracks, I was optimistic. Even the hardshell traditionalists would, I thought, now concede that molecular targeting was the best long-term strategy for drug discovery.

My conviction deepened when I saw the first results from the lovastatin clinical tests in patients with high blood cholesterol. Lovastatin dramatically reduced cholesterol – especially LDL – to a degree never before achieved with a drug. Now the clinical researchers and even the marketing group began to get excited.

Lovastatin sailed through the initial, short-term safety studies with excellent marks, and Merck received a patent in the United States and several countries abroad. Sankyo, which was dogging our steps, had independently discovered an identical compound in Japan (along with compactin) and acquired patent rights in that country and a number of other markets.

Nevertheless, the outlook for lovastatin was marvelous. In small numbers of patients, every additional test indicated that it safely lowered cholesterol levels. Clinical research was beginning to gather the information required before wide-scale studies could begin in humans. This research was ongoing, but the preliminary results looked wonderful to all of us – especially to Al Alberts and me. It seemed almost too good to be true.

\* \* \*

Lovastatin was very much on my mind as I headed to our annual four-day research meeting on a beautiful day in September 1980. Al and Art were quickly pushing ahead with products that made "BLOCKBUSTER" flash into my mind. With MRL on the edge of achieving two major breakthroughs, I was feeling confident about my leadership as my limo drove through the Pine Barrens to the Seaview Resort at Absecon, New Jersey.

Merck's scientists were gathering there to survey the year's accomplishments and plan our new program. I was arriving early because I'd arranged a singles tennis match with my colleague Stan Fidelman. It was a good occasion to have some private time with Stan, who was a close friend and a very special person in our organization.

Every leader should have a person like Stan on his team. When I needed to break down barriers and improve communications, I could always turn to Stan for help. He was an engineer by training and a great communicator. He had worked for Merck since leaving college, and he seemed to know everyone by their first name. His official title was Head of Project Coordination, but his unofficial job was Problem Solver. He knew everything that was going on at Merck, and everyone, literally everyone, liked him.

When I had two groups disagreeing about something, I'd send Stan to find out what the issues *really* were and how to restore peace. He was a knowledgeable mediator. Because they trusted him, people told him things they wouldn't tell anyone else – especially me. Every corporate officer needs a person like Stan who can keep reopening those communications channels that seem to close every time you stop paying attention to them.

After musing about Stan and our approaching tennis match, I began to focus on the meetings and the questions we had to answer. Which programs were making substantial progress? Which had the greatest potential to make an impact on human or animal diseases? Which had the greatest financial potential? How was the effort distributed across the laboratories? Did we have adequate numbers of people? Did they have enough space, equipment, funds? Setting priorities is the key to planning. There are never enough people or funds to do everything, and the goal of the meeting at Seaview was to develop a firm set of priorities.

Since I enjoyed that intellectual challenge, the annual meetings were exciting for me. Our scientists always had late-breaking experimental results that they held back and released at Seaview, hoping to make their project the central attraction of the session. There were always surprises – some compelling, some exciting, some just titillating. These late results always stimulated questions and suggestions from an audience that included the senior members of Merck's laboratories from all over the world.

By the time I was approaching the resort, I had pretty much finished my review and felt good about the reports I had just read. Our improvements in personnel and procedures were making themselves felt throughout the organization. Molecular targeted research was winning converts at both Rahway and West Point. Things were going so well I should have been suspicious. But I wasn't. I was just enjoying the good times and good work as I glided into the resort.

\* \* \*

These intense four-day sessions were one of the forms of communication that helped keep an organization as big as Merck effective over the long haul. A great deal of my time at the laboratories was spent trying to improve communications, formal and informal, inside the division as well as across divisional lines. It might seem easy, but it's not. Most of us tend to fall into a familiar groove, whether at work, at lunch, or at home. Some of the most intense people, those most dedicated to their work, are the least likely to get out of their grooves and meet someone who works on a different project in another building.

At Seaview we had scientists from the major laboratories in Rahway and West Point, but also from our research organization in Canada, many of whom met only at these gatherings. So the meetings were important because they encouraged these intense professionals to get acquainted with colleagues they didn't normally meet day to day. Some of those talks took place in the formal meetings, some in the hallways, some on the tennis court, and some over drinks in the evenings.

Late Monday afternoon, after the first full day of reports and discussions, ten of us, all senior research executives, were doing just that – having drinks and relaxing in the comfortable living room of the presidential suite. We were all in harmony, feeling confident about our programs and Merck's future.

A pharmaceutical company's prospects depend most importantly on what's in the research pipeline. Our major responsibility was to keep our pipeline full, because, in effect, Merck's corporate strategy bet the company's future on the ability of MRL to keep coming up with important new drugs. And not just any drug. Merck periodically needed a blockbuster product in order to grow in a way that would keep the company's top executives and investors happy. That's why they'd recruited me from Washington University.

Two of the company's major products, *Indocin* and *Aldomet*, would be going off patent in the United States in the next year, so there was good cause to be nervous about the immediate future. In 1980 Merck was in better financial condition than most of the nation's businesses, which were being hurt by high interest rates, inflation, and competition from firms in Germany and Japan. But Merck needed at least one blockbuster product soon.

This is why we were all watching lovastatin so closely. We thought it had the potential to become a billion-dollar-a-year product. The results from our initial clinical studies in humans indicated that we had a medical as well as financial breakthrough coming, very soon.

\* \* \*

Then we received a devastating telephone call. The bad news came from Boyd Woodruff, one of our top research executives in Japan, where Merck was doing a substantial business. Woodruff reported that our Japanese competitor, Sankyo, had run aground in its efforts to develop compactin, the cholesterol-lowering agent that was structurally related to lovastatin. According to the story Boyd had heard, the company had stopped its clinical studies in humans because compactin caused tumors in the animals used in the safety assessment tests.

We were stunned. We knew that the Sankyo drug and lovastatin functioned through the same mechanism of action, targeting the same enzyme. If compactin caused tumors because it inhibited this enzyme, then lovastatin might be toxic as well. On the other hand, the toxicity might be due to the unique structure of compactin, which differed from lovastatin. We had no way of knowing which of these possibilities was the case. We only knew that Sankyo had stopped a crucial clinical trial. That alone meant compactin had encountered very serious problems.

As evening fell and the first shock wore off, we launched an intense discussion. How could we verify the rumor? What should we do with the clinical trial of lovastatin? Bert Peltier and Marvin Jaffe, who were responsible for Merck's clinical studies, insisted that we should immediately try to get additional information from Japan. Charlie Leighton, our regulatory expert, was initially too traumatized to say anything. When he recovered, he agreed that we needed to run the rumor to ground. As the discussion continued, the noise level shot up and people began to interrupt one another.

By that point, I thought we had reached three conclusions. First, we should immediately stop all the clinical studies. Second, we should notify the FDA. Finally, I should try to get more information directly from Sankyo. We kept returning to the point that we had seen no evidence, absolutely no indication in our own thorough safety and clinical tests, that lovastatin produced these kinds of effects. Our studies were of relatively short duration, but they had raised no warnings. Nevertheless, we knew we had to move forcefully. The news that Sankyo had actually terminated its clinical trials simply overwhelmed us.

I tried to pump some optimism back into the group. "I'm certain," I said, "that any cancer caused by Sankyo's drug isn't due to a mechanism shared with lovastatin." But the ensuing silence told me I was the only one at the table capable of believing that. My colleagues knew, as I did, that my optimistic hypothesis was one of two possibilities, and none of us had the evidence that evening to decide which one was correct.

Only one thing seemed certain at that moment: Merck had to stop its clinical trials immediately, and that's what I did. Jaffe left to phone the physicians in charge of the trials to tell them to stop their programs at once. Charlie Leighton went to phone the FDA. If I hadn't been trained as a physician, I might have been tempted to waffle a bit on this decision. If I'd been the nervous president of a small start-up company with only one drug candidate in development, I'm certain the decision would have been more difficult to make. Then I might have tried to reassure myself, mulling over the fact that lovastatin had easily cleared all of the hurdles in Merck's early safety assessment tests.

I knew how our professionals in safety assessment approached their job, going after each compound with the goal of doing everything possible to make certain that any potential toxicity would be identified. The worst thing to do would be to allow a compound to move forward into human clinical trials and then discover it was toxic. Lovastatin had sailed through short-term safety assessment with no indication whatsoever that it might produce tumors. We knew, however, that Merck had not completed all of the long-term toxicology studies, and that left a dark cloud of doubt in our minds.

I left to call John Horan, Merck's chairman and CEO. I explained the rumor, its implications for lovastatin, and my decision. Horan, who immediately understood the gravity of this situation, agreed that we had no choice but to stop the trials. He asked to be kept informed.

Later, having moved into the bar, our little group was still absolutely stunned, unable to say anything new or encouraging. "I'll contact Sankyo directly," I repeated, "and find out whether the rumor's true. At this point, all we've got is a thirdhand report." This promise didn't pump them up any more than my previous try had.

Before I could call Sankyo, however, I had to make a more difficult phone call. I had to tell Al Alberts what had happened. The conversation was painful. "Al," I said, "I've just heard from Boyd Woodruff that Sankyo's stopped clinical trials on its cholesterol compound. Apparently it caused tumors in the safety tests." There was a long silence on the other end of the line. Very few pharmaceutical researchers ever get as close as he was to discovering a major drug. Hardly any has that experience more than once in a career. After a moment to collect his thoughts, he tried to find a compromise position, hoping his project wouldn't go dead in the water.

"Let's find another molecule," I replied, "one with a structure different enough from compactin that they cannot possibly have similar toxicities." But we both knew that wouldn't enable Al's project to keep its momentum. When we stopped the clinical studies, our head of clinical research would tell investigating physicians that our compound was "presumed" to cause cancer – at least in the animals used in safety assessment. Until we learned otherwise, we would assume the report from Japan was true and that lovastatin might have a similar problem.

\* \* \*

MRL had now suffered a devastating setback, and it wasn't easy to jack up morale after the meetings. We'd been following the research approach I'd advocated, concentrating a high percentage of our scientific resources on our most promising compounds. Now we had to accept the fact that we'd probably lost our most outstanding example of drug discovery based on molecular targeting. Was the strategy wrong?

That dreary winter in Rahway, the strategy question kept running through our minds as the months dragged by. We went through the motions of doing research, but we were unable to recover the pace we'd lost with the phone call from Japan. We accelerated the search for an alternative to lovastatin. Our chemists had high hopes that this time *they'd* be able to develop an effective cholesterol-lowering compound, but their initial explorations were not encouraging. Meanwhile, we pressed ahead with toxicology studies, none of which eventually corroborated the story from Japan. But full toxicology results come only after the long-term tests are finished, and they were still in the works.

When an organization goes flat, its worst aspects begin to look more and more prominent. At MRL we had made considerable progress in improving communications, but after we put the "hold" order on lovastatin, we could see only what we hadn't achieved in this regard.

We still hadn't, for instance, been able to bridge the fault line between basic research and clinical operations. The clinical staff still tended to take hold of a compound and cut off discussions with the scientists who had developed it. The attitude on the clinical side was "Now it's our baby, and as soon as we've finished our work, we'll talk to you about our results." I kept urging them to communicate regularly, to share ideas, but deeply rooted practices are hard to change. This is especially true when they're reinforced by a sense of competition, a touch of jealousy about who gets credit for the discovery, and a powerful desire to protect your professional turf. This made us less effective than we could have been.

We struggled to get moving again, but I was not at all satisfied with our progress or with my own efforts as president of MRL. All I had to do was read the company's *Annual Report* that year to be deeply concerned. For those who could read between the lines, the report gave too much attention to improvements in sales of older products, including some that were obviously mature and experiencing "moderate growth." Instead of highlighting a new blockbuster, we were touting "continued solid acceptance of our established products...."

When I looked at the report, I wanted to tell everyone, "WE JUST NEED MORE TIME!" But obviously I couldn't do that. In the meantime, the report in effect told our employees, the public, and investors that Merck either hadn't broken out of a flat period or was encountering a major internal problem, or both.

At another company, I might have seen my job as well as lovastatin and the promising new approach to drug discovery all go in the tank together. Fortunately, at Merck there was a good understanding of the problematic nature of innovation in pharmaceuticals. CEO John Horan was obviously disappointed when I told him about the problems with lovastatin, but he never tried to alter our strategic objectives in research. He and the Board of Directors continued to provide solid support for MRL.

Despite the crisis, they gave me additional responsibilities and in addition to being head of the labs, I became a corporate senior vice president for strategic planning. The opportunity to oversee planning for the entire corporation tossed me into a new arena. As I began to dig into that job, I realized for the first time just how complex Merck was and how many needs in addition to new products the company had to satisfy. I was pleased to be promoted, but nothing of that sort could make up for our problems with lovastatin. I had twenty-five years of intense research riding on that project, and it was a gloomy time for me and for the entire research organization at Merck.

\* \* \*

Then we caught a break. In 1982, Roger Illingworth of Portland, Oregon, a prominent heart specialist, and two fellow cardiologists from Dallas were visiting Merck as consultants to give us an outside perspective on our programs at the laboratories. In their clinical practices all three were treating patients with serious heart disease, their coronary arteries narrowed by plaques of cholesterol and fat. Not coincidentally, these patients had elevated cholesterol and LDL cholesterol levels that hadn't responded to any of the available treatments. The three clinicians were in complete agreement: They wanted to use lovastatin on high-risk patients. Illingworth, Grundy, and his colleague David Bilheimer were eager to restart limited clinical trials because the outlook for their patients was dire.

I knew they were right. As the head of Merck's research labs, I was tempted but hesitant. The evidence these and other medical researchers had uncovered pointed to elevated cholesterol levels as a major cause of heart disease, and I knew that the high-risk patients Grundy, Bilheimer, and Illingworth were treating had been unable to bring their cholesterol levels down to a safe range either through diets or drugs. In many such cases, badly clogged arteries left the patients facing almost certain encounters with heart attacks and death.

Still, I was hesitant to move back into clinical trials, and this request led to an extended bout of soul searching. I'd been unable to confirm the reports from Japan. But I couldn't just ignore them. That was why we'd launched extensive toxicology tests in animals, looking for any evidence that lovastatin might have similar effects. All the studies had produced favorable results. One of them, a two-year analysis, wasn't completed, but we already had in hand a substantial body of evidence indicating that lovastatin was safe.[3] We were forced to balance the hoped-for benefits of lower cholesterol against the possibility that these high-risk patients would suffer adverse side effects from the drug.

Convinced that we should move ahead, we assembled all of the information we'd collected and presented it to the FDA. The agency agreed with our evaluation and authorized trials in high-risk patients. Al Alberts, who had never lost confidence in lovastatin, his first major "hit," was excited when I told him we were restarting clinical tests. As the good news raced through MRL, it boosted the morale of the entire organization. Al told me, deadpan, that he knew all along we wouldn't find anything wrong with his favorite molecule. Beneath the kidding and excitement, everyone at Merck understood all too clearly that we were actually holding our breath as lovastatin began its second trip into clinical research.

---

[3] The two-year study ultimately established that lovastatin did not have the adverse affects which concerned us.

All the time that lovastatin had been on the sidelines, I had been pushing Al and his team of biologists and chemists to come up with another molecule that wouldn't be plagued by toxicity. Although this seemed straightforward at the start, the search had turned out to be difficult and frustrating. Still, we kept the pressure on even when lovastatin went back to clinical research. Finally, Bob Smith and his chemists designed a second inhibitor (simvastatin). We brought this new drug along as quickly as possible so it could serve either as a backup candidate if lovastatin ran into problems or as a second Merck entry into a huge potential market.

Just as our renewed clinical research was getting under way, the National Heart, Lung, and Blood Institute published a landmark study on the relationship between cholesterol levels and coronary artery disease. The Institute's findings confirmed what we'd long suspected on the basis of the earlier epidemiological data. For every percentage point the level of elevated cholesterol is reduced, the chance of heart attack is cut by about two percentage points.

By this time, however, we weren't thinking about one or two percentage points. Our clinical tests were showing reductions of 18 to 34 percent in total cholesterol, with higher figures for the most dangerous (LDL) form of cholesterol. Lovastatin was also pushing up the levels of high-density lipoprotein cholesterol (HDL), which helps protect arteries against elevated levels of LDL.[4]

Our confidence about lovastatin was growing, even though we knew it wasn't a "perfect drug." All drugs have side effects, some of which are dangerous. Even aspirin has side effects. Some drugs have to be taken so frequently or in such large amounts that patients find it hard to stay on the regimen. Some drugs can be

---

[4] Our new drug was also reducing blood triglycerides, which would also be good news for persons threatened with coronary artery disease.

administered only in a hospital or doctor's office. Lovastatin was different. By taking one pill once a day, many patients would be able to bring their cholesterol under control with minimal side effects.

Our trials demonstrated that most of the side effects were mild. Most passed quickly, and fewer than 1 percent of the patients had to drop out of the trials. Some (2%) experienced an increase in liver enzymes, but most of these were patients taking higher doses, and we recommended that physicians monitor them. Lovastatin also caused some muscle damage in rare instances, but these side effects were reversed when the drug was stopped. By the time all of our clinical results were in, I was pleased with the findings. Lovastatin was well tolerated, safe, and extremely effective in reducing a major risk factor in cardiovascular disease.

When the FDA officially approved lovastatin, which became the pathbreaking drug *Mevacor* in 1987, Merck celebrated the event with the customary press conference. For Al Alberts and me, however, the real celebration had taken place many months before, when we studied the initial findings of the clinical tests and reflected on the decades we'd spent together working our way along the path that led to this new therapy.

With FDA approval, Merck could at last start marketing *Mevacor*, and, as we knew, about half of America's middle-aged adults had cholesterol levels that increased their risk of heart disease. In this country alone, there were about a million and a half heart attacks every year. We thought *Mevacor*, which was the first statin marketed anywhere in the world, would make a telling dent in those figures, enabling millions of people to live longer, better lives. That was a rich moment for both of us.

\* \* \*

66

Before all of those good results could flow out of the *Mevacor* discovery, however, Merck's marketing division (MSD) had to get to work and promote the drug. That, as it turned out, was not a simple matter. There were still many skeptics in the medical profession and university medical departments. All we had was epidemiological evidence indicating that a high incidence of death from heart attacks was correlated with high cholesterol levels. For some physicians, this was still a "cholesterol hypothesis."

We were in the same position as those early researchers who thought they could demonstrate that smoking tobacco caused cancer. They could show a statistical relationship and actually tell you your odds of dying from cancer if you continued smoking. They'd shown that cigarette smokers who quit were less likely to develop lung cancer than those who kept smoking. But the tobacco researchers still couldn't demonstrate at the molecular level how, exactly, tobacco smoke caused normal lung cells to be transformed into cancerous ones.

I was as certain that smoking caused lung cancer as I was that high cholesterol levels caused heart attacks. If you looked at populations with high cholesterol, it was apparent that the probability of their dying from heart attack was far higher than populations who had low cholesterol levels. That was good enough evidence for me, the National Institutes of Health, and the American Heart Association. It was also convincing evidence for those physicians in the United States and other countries who quickly began to prescribe *Mevacor*.

However, the skeptics still weren't convinced. So we pushed ahead with research, and a few years later we were able to release the results of a five-year study of over 4,400 patients using Merck's second statin *Zocor* (simvastatin). All of these people already had coronary heart disease, having experienced a heart attack or suffered the intensely painful choking sensation, "angina pectoris," that results from narrowed coronary arteries. They all had high cholesterol as well.

The findings this time astonished even those of us who had anticipated favorable results for patients taking Merck's therapy. The drug cut overall mortality by an incredible 30 percent. Deaths by coronary occlusion were reduced by 42 percent, and the need for coronary surgery was decreased by 37 percent. Strokes, which can be caused by occlusion of an artery in the brain, were reduced by 30 percent. In addition, the drug's use led to lower overall health care costs.

The "cholesterol hypothesis" had now been converted to fact. We'd established decisively that lower levels of cholesterol meant there would be less narrowing of coronary arteries and shown that overall mortality was reduced. These findings and the direct experiences of physicians prescribing our drug produced a snowball effect. Soon *Mevacor* and *Zocor* combined had over half of the market in the United States for cholesterol-lowering agents and were being used in more than thirty other countries.[5]

We had a billion-dollar-a-year therapy in hand. Sales of *Mevacor* and *Zocor* soared around the world. To put this in context, bear in mind that Merck's annual sales for all its products – including specialty chemicals – had not broken $1 billion until 1973, just

---

[5] After our competitors targeted the same enzyme and invented their own inhibitors, the resulting struggles for market share were fierce and not always fair. Competition normally has positive results in this and other industries, but sometimes our competitors launched negative "rumor campaigns," claiming for instance that Merck's product caused sleeplessness. We saw no evidence of this in our clinical studies or in the market, but we were concerned. So we did a short-term clinical trial of potential sleep effects with half the patients on *Mevacor* and the other half taking a placebo. The results of this test and subsequent research established that sleeplessness was not a problem.

two years before I'd joined the Merck Research Laboratories. So *Mevacor* was big news in the firm, the industry, and the investment community as well as in medical circles in the United States and abroad.

*Mevacor* was all the more exciting because it was part of a great wave of new products that came through the Merck pipeline in the 1980s. It was this wave and the way that Merck was able to take advantage of it that moved the company to the top of the global pharmaceutical industry. Merck became the leading innovator in global pharmaceuticals.

*Vasotec*, the high-blood-pressure drug that Art Patchett championed, was another important part of our success story. Scientists at Squibb had synthesized a chemical that inhibited a specific enzyme – ACE – which is part of the body's regulatory system for controlling blood pressure.[6] Squibb's prototype inhibitor could be administered only intravenously, so they continued their research and invented captopril, which they sold as *Capoten*, a drug that could be taken orally.

This line of research was especially exciting to Art Patchett, as it gave him an opportunity to return to his earlier work on the high-blood-pressure problem. As with *Mevacor*, the targeted enzyme was involved in a complex sequence that scientists had been studying for many years. So in both instances, we were looking for a single molecule that would, with minimal side effects, inhibit and thus control a vital biochemical process. As our understanding of the specific enzyme improved, so too did our odds of finding an effective inhibitor.

We decided to try to improve on the Squibb product. We diagrammed the captopril molecule, and several of us recognized that

---

[6] ACE refers to the angiotensin-converting enzyme.

one element of it was likely to be a significant source of side effects. MRL was familiar with this element from some of its other work, as I was from my biochemical research.[7] After pondering this situation a bit, I suggested to Art that if he could make an inhibitor that lacked this element, he'd have a winner because we already knew captopril worked in humans. Art and our other chemists were so talented at designing molecules that I was indeed certain they could do this.

This prompted Art to give his boss another lesson in chemistry. He had given me a number before in less stressful situations. Now he explained patiently that the element we were trying to get rid of played a vital role by combining with an essential metal in the active site of the enzyme we were trying to inhibit. This, he said, made his job complicated and problematic.

As the months passed, Art proved correct about the difficulty. Merck Research had tremendous resources, and we gave Art and his group all of the help they could use. But still it took them about a year to work out the solution. What they finally invented was the compound enalapril, which became *Vasotec*, a safe, effective means of reducing high blood pressure.

*Vasotec*, we found, had a big, unexpected advantage. We hadn't tried for a once-a-day drug, but we got one.[8] Clinical trials showed *Vasotec* to be long-acting, and physicians recognize that

[7] The element was the sulfhydryl group.
[8] While Art was working to design a drug that lacked the problem element of *Capoten*, publications from Squibb revealed the side effects we had anticipated. For a short period we were excited that our drug would have an advantage since it would lack those side effects. Then, further studies of *Capoten* showed that this drug, taken at lower doses, would not show these side effects. So the predicted advantage of *Vasotec* vanished. However, in order to normalize blood pressure throughout the day and night with lower doses, *Capoten* had to be taken two or three times per day.

compliance with long-term therapy is much more effective when their patients take their drug only once a day. As a result, when we finally got it out, *Vasotec* quickly took a huge share of the market. It beat *Mevacor* to market and indeed became the first billion-dollar drug in Merck's history.

*Vasotec* provides an outstanding example of the benefits of so-called me-too innovation in pharmaceuticals (and, from my point-of-view, every other industry). Our new product was important to Merck and to millions of patients because we had persisted in seeking an improved drug. So long as the objective of your research is to make an improved drug, "me-too" research is just research. That's what competition is all about. Allowing that process to continue has helped make the American pharmaceutical industry the world's leader in new drug development. The critics of "me-too" innovation are simply wrong.

\* \* \*

During the same years that MRL was developing important new cardiovascular drugs, our laboratories were also making great progress in antibiotics. Antibiotics are an important area of drug discovery, but they are an accountant's nightmare because their development is so unpredictable and involves such long-term expenditures. Most of the world's antibiotics – including ours – were discovered by testing soil samples for microorganisms that make substances that stop the growth of bacteria. This sounds easy, but there is of course a catch. The discovery process is inherently random, and it may take five or ten years to find the right soil sample and isolate the right active substance in it. This search may take even longer than a decade.

Although slow and erratic, the research is of vital interest to society because the evolution of resistant forms of bacteria means we are in an unending life-and-death struggle. The medical community has actually fostered resistance by overprescribing antibiotics. Physicians have, for instance, used these drugs to treat the common cold or other viral infections – infections that don't respond to antibiotics. All too soon, this led to the evolution of mutant forms of bacteria that were drug-resistant. This made it all the more important that Merck and other companies keep sifting thousands of soil samples in their "discovery screens" to find nature's antimicrobial substances.

In one instance, it took Merck ten years of research to develop a single new antibiotic, *Mefoxin*. When I arrived in Rahway in 1975, Merck's scientists had already discovered *Mefoxin*, but then we had to figure out how to develop and market it. It had been more than twenty years since the company had found a new antibiotic, so no one in our marketing and sales division had any experience with this type of product. This time we had to look outside the firm, hiring new personnel who understood the antibiotics market. Merck quickly built up a hospital sales force and got our new antibiotic off to a running start. Their successful efforts helped to make *Mefoxin* the number one hospital antibiotic for years.

But, of course, the Darwinian struggle continued and new antibiotics were eventually needed to confront resistant microbes. Our next successful effort to beat back infection was the discovery of thienamycin. The active substance in this case was extremely unstable. With great effort, we succeeded in purifying it and determining its structure. Then our chemists were able to develop a stable derivative (imipenem), but the new compound couldn't be produced in amounts that would make it commercially viable.

This time, the chemists, led by Burt Christensen, scored a great triumph. They finally solved the production problem by coming up with the first totally synthetic process for making an antibiotic in Merck's history. It was probably the most complex synthesis in the history of the industry, and it made possible large-scale production of a compound that was actually a better antibiotic than the original natural substance we'd discovered.[9]

The resulting drug, *Primaxin*, was effective against more disease-causing bacteria than any other drug on the market at that time (1985). It was so effective, in fact, that many hospitals held it in reserve as the final line of defense against infections that wouldn't respond to other drugs. Its nickname was "gorillamycin."

* * *

MRL's success in new drug development pushed Merck to the top of the fast-growing pharmaceutical industry in the United States. And by the early 1980s America was the world leader in pharmaceutical innovation. Other countries had made and were continuing to make vital contributions to the basic science foundation for applied research. But the United States had leapt ahead in the process of converting biochemical science into products that would contribute to human health.

My contribution to Merck's enhanced role in global pharmaceuticals was to pursue with determination a strategy of drug discovery consistent with the latest innovations in biochemistry and enzymology. Along the way, I worked hard to improve every department in MRL, to upgrade our personnel, and to focus our resources on the most promising drug candidates. I prioritized my efforts every day and tried to run an organization that had a sure grip on its own primary goals.

[9] The antibiotic was combined with an enzyme inhibitor that prevented its inactivation by the body.

I had learned from each one of my mistakes, all of which I had pondered at some length. Now at last I was willing to give myself a higher grade as an R&D leader, but curiously, MRL's success made it inevitable that Diana and I would start looking for another ten-year plan.

# CHAPTER FIVE

# Corporate Grooming

A S MY TEN-YEAR ANNIVERSARY AS HEAD OF THE MERCK
Research Laboratories approached, Diana and I realized
we were facing another turning point in our lives. Several Merck
projects were coming to fruition. Most of our research and development teams now had strong leadership. As I passed my fifty-
third birthday, Diana and I began to talk through our next big
career move.

The desire to move on was rooted in success, as it had been
before. We'd left NIH when my team's basic research in enzymology had brought us to the front of an intensely competitive
field. Later, Diana and I had left Washington University because
we agreed that we'd accomplished our major goals together. At
that time, we faced a new situation in corporate research and
development – something we'd never done and never even imag-
ined doing. But we were certain it was important, not just to us,
but to all those who would benefit from the drugs we might help
Merck discover. Once we had *Mevacor* moving toward completion, *Vasotec* ready to go, and other therapies pushing through the

pipeline, it was clear to both of us that we'd pretty much achieved the goal that had brought us to Merck.

Merck Research Laboratories was, I thought, the best in the industry, that is, the global industry. We weren't the quickest organization because we set very high standards for our products and were convinced that we didn't have to cut corners on any part of the R&D process to be successful. Throughout the laboratories, there was now a powerful sense of accomplishment that reinforced the dedication to our new style of drug discovery. Targeted research had proven itself.

I wanted to keep MRL on top, so I had worked hard at replacing myself. I had started looking for a successor as early as 1981, long before I was ready to leave my job. I understood how important it was to have a good succession plan. The pressure of daily events keeps you from thinking about replacing yourself, but you need to keep this problem up near the top of your priority list because the process can be lengthy.

First I had to decide whether we had a potential successor among the senior people in MRL. We clearly had great strength in several scientific disciplines, including my specialties, biochemistry and enzymology. While it would have been easy to find a new leader in biochemistry, I would, in effect, have been trying to clone myself. That approach seems to be pleasing to many executives. But I think that's how some of America's largest and most successful businesses faltered when they began to feel the pressure of foreign competition. Instead of looking for new leaders who could take their organizations in different directions, the top executives promoted people who'd be certain to stay on the same path that had carried their firms to the top. But, of course, that trail no longer led to the top.

I decided Merck needed a research leader who could develop MRL's capabilities in some of the most promising newer areas of research: molecular genetics and recombinant DNA technology. He or she should be able to do this while continuing to utilize the laboratories' proven strengths in chemistry, biochemistry, enzymology, and virology.

Our strategy was explicit. We wanted to take advantage of molecular genetics to help identify protein molecules that were promising targets for chemical attack. But with some exceptions such as the hepatitis B vaccine and a few other projects, we still didn't want to use the new technology to make proteins. Proteins are large molecules that have to be injected (usually in a physician's office or hospital). Our goal was to continue discovering enzyme inhibitors or receptor antagonists that were smaller molecules which would be active and effective when taken orally.

Used this way, the new technology and science would complement perfectly what we had built up during the previous seven years. At that time, however, we had no scientist in molecular genetics of the stature and experience called for by this job. So we looked outside of Merck.

We found a promising candidate in Ed Scolnick, a distinguished physician scientist. Like me, Ed had been an intern and resident at Mass General and then gone on to the National Institutes of Health. I'd been trying for some years to increase the number of M.D. scientists throughout our laboratories. Merck's central mission was the development of new treatments of disease, and I thought it was easier for scientists who had been through medical school and had some clinical experience to make connections between new developments in science and drug discovery. They also had a better feel for different diseases and the effects they have on people because they recognized firsthand the shortcomings of available therapies.

Although Scolnick and I had these experiences in common, he was no clone. In most other regards, he and I had chosen different paths into medical science. Right from the start, Ed had been intrigued by molecular genetics. He was my junior by about ten or eleven years, and in that decade, gene-based science had become a more exciting biological frontier than biochemistry and enzymology. Both were thriving, but by the early 1980s, molecular genetics was newer and hotter. At the National Cancer Institute of the NIH, cancer research had become Ed's lifetime obsession.

By the early 1980s, Scolnick had collected a number of major awards for distinguished scientific contributions. He had breadth as well as depth. I knew he'd be the kind of high energy science leader who would stay personally engaged with the wide variety of projects under way at MRL. I persuaded him to join our laboratory in 1982, starting out as head of research in Virus and Cell Biology under Maurice Hilleman, who was scheduled to retire shortly. Scolnick saw Merck's recombinant vaccine against hepatitis B through to completion, which was a difficult task for a scientist who had no previous experience with the practical aspects of vaccine development.

Ed knew from the beginning that I was grooming him to take on the responsibilities of running our large R&D organization. I was confident that whenever I left and wherever I went, the laboratories would be positioned to take full advantage of their existing strengths while building new capabilities in recombinant technology and in Scolnick's style of molecular genetics. With this blend of new and established talents, I thought we might even be able to conquer the deadly retrovirus that we knew was causing AIDS.

\* \* \*

By that time, around 1984, Diana and I knew exactly what we wanted my next job to be. We just didn't know where it would be. After acquiring some new responsibilities outside the laboratories during the last few years at Merck, I'd become intrigued by what made the company tick. And what might make it tick even better.

I still found some aspects of the business world distressing, but I loved the competition and still do. It brought out the best in me and, I've observed, in most of us. Competition is what keeps my juices running, and I'm absolutely convinced it's what keeps capitalism productive and efficient. That's why we decided it was time for a third career, preferably as CEO of a pharmaceutical firm and preferably at Merck, whose corporate culture and operations were compatible with our values. But if not Merck, then another leading firm in the industry.

During my first six years at MRL, I'd kept a tight focus on the researchers and their programs, not on the corporation as such. My primary concern had been developing new therapies, not making money. I appreciated the significance of a billion-dollar drug, and I knew we were in the business of producing pharmaceuticals, not science. But my passion was the solution of significant medical problems, not corporate problems.

I understood that a reasonable board member might have concluded that Roy Vagelos didn't have the right mind-set to become Merck's CEO. My résumé was missing a few items that any board of directors worth its salt would want to see. For starters, I'd never taken a course in business. Or accounting. Or business law. As late as 1982, my résumé announced that I had never displayed the slightest interest in being a business executive.

Although I'd been running a research organization with a $300 million annual budget, I still had only the most rudimentary knowledge of accounting procedures. I'd gratefully left the business details to the financial experts, whose efforts let me focus on the work at the labs.

Despite these handicaps, John Horan, Merck's chairman and CEO, began giving me opportunities to fill some of the holes in my résumé. He set out to develop and to test my ability as a line officer – a senior vice president as of 1982 – handling a broader range of responsibilities and people. I was grooming and being groomed at the same time.

Once again, I found myself on the steep part of the learning curve, taking home stacks of reading material in order to pass this new "course." Once again, I had an instructor. Frank Spiegel was my guide to the mysteries of the corporate world. Frank and I were thrown together when we began to share responsibility for strategic planning for the corporation.

Merck's planning process was no mystery, even for a scientist trying to learn on the job. Once a year, Frank collected strategic plans from each division and staff group. These projections were for the coming year, and the plans generally looked forward to improvements in performance. I knew all about these divisional reports because I'd been doing them since becoming president of MRL in 1976.

In the labs, our annual projections were always conservative. In these matters and, in fact, in anything involving budgets, I've never overcome my upbringing during the Great Depression. As a result, I'm an instinctive fiscal conservative with an intense desire to see each case grounded as solidly as possible in hard data. Having no flair for "boosterism," I submitted brutally honest projections for the laboratories. I didn't want more money. I wanted more output. As I understood my job, it was to make my operations more efficient, not just bigger.

When Frank started walking me through the reports from the other divisions and the staff, however, I learned that not everyone took the projections seriously and not all of them were conservative about the future. Some divisions seemed to approach the process as a bureaucratic game. The international group's motto was "THINK BIG!" They provided outlandish projections, which prompted me to ask the leaders of the division, "Do you believe these numbers?" "Oh no," was the reply, "but it gives the people in our division something to hope for." The domestic pharmaceutical division apparently needed less "hope" because they played the game differently. By turning in very low projections, they tried to ensure that they'd always exceed top management's expectations.

I began to recognize that the basic strategy was predetermined – deeply rooted in Merck's history. Actually, I could now see that CEO Henry Gadsden had explained it to me before I accepted Merck's offer to head the labs. In effect, his successor, Horan, had reaffirmed it every year when he looked at my budget for MRL. The CEO always approved my budget requests without asking difficult questions. Why? So far as I could tell, it was in part because our requests were conservative and in part because MRL was the centerpiece of Merck's strategic plan.

Since the 1930s, Merck had been investing heavily in research. The founder's son, George W. Merck, had launched this policy innovation, and all of the subsequent CEOs had followed the same basic strategy, looking to the labs to provide the new patented products that would enable the company to keep growing. From time to time, the CEOs added something special to the strategic plan: John Connor (1955–65) emphasized expansion overseas – first in Latin America and then in Europe. After Henry Gadsden (1965–76) became convinced the federal government would impose price controls on pharmaceuticals, he started a modest diversification plan to hedge against controls, guarding in effect against reduced profit margins in prescription drugs. John Horan (1976–85) built up Merck's operations in the Far East, especially Japan. But all of these strategic additions were secondary to research, which was always Merck's first priority.

When the company added something to its strategy, it was usually a target of opportunity, not a product of formal long-range planning. In the early 1980s, Merck's corporate strategy continued to evolve in this incremental, ad hoc fashion, and I didn't try to change that pattern of development or the role of the divisional projections in the process. I didn't think I could. I nudged the CEO once or twice, but for the most part, Frank Spiegel and I just massaged the numbers and kept cranking out the kind of reports Merck had been producing for many years.

I could see that there were reasons to introduce a different approach to planning. We could, for instance, have taken the process out of the hands of the departments and divisions and introduced elements they were overlooking such as changes in the regulatory environment. But I didn't think I could muster the support needed to change that aspect of the company's operations.

So I spent my time learning as much about the business side of pharmaceuticals as I could from Frank Spiegel and from visits to the marketing, sales, and manufacturing divisions. There I learned that the divisions were actually pursuing their own long-term strategies, which they weren't sharing with the corporate planners, who were considered extraneous.

\* \* \*

Marketing interested me because soon after joining MRL, one of the top marketing executives had said, "Roy, you have to understand that this company is used to breakthroughs. That's what we're used to selling." I mulled that over for a long time. I thought every physician wanted to give patients the best drugs, even if they were only modest improvements over current therapies. Surely that's what all patients wanted too. I thought our marketing organization should be strong enough to promote a drug that might be the third in its class to reach the market but represented important improvements, or even a modest improvement, over the competition. I began to tuck these ideas away for future use along with the other things I learned about marketing.

The scientists at Merck looked down on marketing as an inferior, low-status activity. Marketing was at best a necessary evil in a company whose glorious accomplishments all came out of the laboratories. Or so they believed – with some justification. At Merck, the scientists were industrial royalty and the marketing folks were commoners. These ideas and the related status hierarchy were so deeply ingrained that marketing personnel were never allowed to take part in MRL meetings.

I quickly decided that was a mistake and asked Stan Fidelman, my "Chief Problem Solver," to help bring the two groups closer together. This was a serious business because I was trying to change Merck's corporate class system. I wanted research and marketing to work together, to communicate with less effort, to work toward our common goal, which was to get the best medicines into the hands of people who needed them.

With Stan negotiating each step in the process, we managed to achieve our goal incrementally. We started by inviting marketing representatives to attend the meetings but to sit away from the table around the borders of the room. They could listen but were not allowed to talk. After the researchers and marketers became accustomed to being in the same room, marketing was at last given a voice. They could comment and actually make suggestions, some of which proved to be extremely important. They told us, for example, what kind of clinical information would help promote particular products. We still didn't allow marketing people to participate in meetings in which we determined which basic research projects MRL should bet on. But on other matters, marketing and research began to communicate more frequently, and the tension between the two groups gradually began to subside.

One of the unanticipated consequences was the respect that more and more of the scientists – including me – began to have for Merck's style of marketing. "Fair balance," invented by John Horan, was the key concept. Merck's marketing and sales people were taught to explain the weaknesses as well as the strengths of our products. By the time I joined the company, the marketing and sales crews were devoted to achieving "fair balance" in everything they did, and I thought they were the best in the industry at making an evenhanded, informative sales pitch.

Like most good business ideas, Horan's concept was both simple and important. After leaving medical school, most physicians have little time to read, and thus drug company marketing personnel become their major source of information about new therapies. Otherwise, they'd just go on prescribing the compounds they'd learned to use in med school – ten, twenty, thirty years before. A pharmaceutical company's marketing and sales force is therefore constantly tempted to exaggerate either the high quality of its own products or the low quality of competing drugs.

In most industries, exaggerating the benefits of your own product and demeaning a competitor's isn't particularly harmful. If a salesperson tells you Coke is better than Pepsi for quenching your thirst, he may or may not be right – but the choice won't seriously affect your health. The pharmaceutical industry is entirely different. Whether the drug works or has side effects can have a decisive impact on people's lives, and a busy physician is likely to choose between two or three possible treatments on the basis of a five-minute conversation with a pharmaceutical representative who leaves him or her a handful of free samples and some literature that may or may not get read.

Merck used those five minutes to present accurate, balanced information about its products. Every piece of paper leaving the company was subjected to a Medical-Legal Review. Every pharmaceutical rep was drilled in the proper procedures. "Fair balance" was deeply ingrained in the company culture. The reward system didn't look just at sales figures but assessed the ability of sales and marketing people to present balanced information. If anything, Merck was overly stringent in what it allowed its people to say. But the great advantage was that, if you worked for Merck, you knew your firm wasn't disseminating dangerous misinformation. You could sleep well.

While I had a deep appreciation for "fair balance," I began to see there were opportunities to strengthen the company's marketing. We had to be more innovative and also adjust more quickly to changes in the marketplace. We certainly had to be able to market products offering modest advantages, even when they weren't "breakthroughs."

By 1984, when the grooming process accelerated, I had tucked into my mind quite a few ideas about the pharmaceutical business. I was increasingly interested in tackling a senior executive position that would enable me to introduce some of the changes I had in mind. CEO John Horan seemed to be satisfied with my progress. At least that was the way I interpreted my promotion that year to executive vice president (EVP).

I had to interpret the significance of the promotion myself because no one told me what, exactly, was going on. The CEO and I were friends but not confidants. All John Horan said when I was promoted was "Roy, I'd like to have your input to these manufacturing and marketing groups. I'd like them to report to you." I said, "Fine. I'd like to learn that part of the business." I didn't ask any questions. He must have assumed that, if I was smart enough to be a candidate for the top position, I should be smart enough to understand why he was giving me some experience as an operating officer. As an EVP, I was now directly responsible for Merck's pharmaceutical, animal health, and specialty chemical divisions as well as research.

This appointment jumped me over the other candidates for the top job. There are almost always at least three or four possible successors, and that was the case at Merck in the mid-1980s. Like most large U.S. corporations, Merck was organized into divisions and functional departments, and the CEO normally looks to the senior executives heading those operations when he or she starts to think about retirement. Customarily, the CEO chooses and the Board of Directors approves. The process resembles the role the U.S. Senate plays in setting foreign policy. The Board, like the Senate, gives its advice and consent, but the real power usually rests with the CEO, who should by that time have carefully weeded out the nonstarters and carefully groomed the leading candidate.

If the CEO is considering an executive in a staff position, this process usually involves a stint in operations. That, I assumed, was why Horan had promoted me and given me responsibilities in marketing, sales, and manufacturing. I also became one of the three company representatives on the Board along with CEO John Horan and President John Huck.

I already knew that we had an excellent Board composed of accomplished people with knowledge and experience in corporate enterprise. They had good judgment, did their homework, and were able to contribute to the firm's success. Some knew the pharmaceutical business; some were more familiar with other industries. They were willing to speak their minds and could not be cowed by management to approve policies they opposed. For instance, they flatly turned down management's proposal to diversify further by acquiring a medical equipment firm.

Merck's Board included people like Dr. Richard S. Ross, for many years the respected Dean of the Medical Faculty at Johns Hopkins. Ross thoroughly understood the medical side of our business, and like many of his colleagues on the Board, knew how to ask tough questions. Another long-term member was Dr. Jacques Genest from the Clinical Research Institute of Montreal, who had a good grasp of what we were trying to achieve at MRL. From business, we had Frank T. Cary of IBM, Dr. Ruben F. Mettler of TRW, and John K. McKinley of Texaco, among others. Al Merck represented the family on the Board, and former Merck CEO John T. Connor also participated.

\* \* \*

As I jumped into my new EVP role, I landed right in the middle of a bitter dispute with organized labor. Top management and the Board were taking a tough position on Merck's contract with the Oil, Chemical, and Atomic Workers Union. The contract had already expired, and, in early May 1984, Merck instructed its union employees not to report to work. The result was a nasty, prolonged struggle that continued into early September 1984.

I agreed completely with the company's position. Over the years, management had avoided work stoppages by making concessions to the unions, gradually allowing its wages and fringe benefits to get far out of line with those of its competitors in pharmaceuticals and with other businesses around Merck plants. Many American corporations had done the same thing and been crippled by competition from more efficient, lower-cost foreign producers. That hadn't happened to Merck. But it didn't take a crystal ball to see that industry conditions were changing dramatically and that the future would bring downward pressure on prices and costs.

I'd already learned enough about the business side of pharmaceuticals to know that Merck would need to operate its plants more efficiently in the next ten years than it had in the past decade. Managed care and the rise of large buying organizations were already supplanting the kinds of individual physician services long familiar to Americans. These new organizations put downward pressure on prices, and that pressure was certain to increase. If Merck didn't respond effectively to these changes, even the best performance by the labs wouldn't protect the company or the workers' jobs.

I also sympathized with the employees and their families. Given my background and my experiences in Estelle's Luncheonette, I understood their feelings about a large corporation that seemed extremely wealthy. But sympathy couldn't change the fact that over the long term neither the workers nor the company would benefit if Merck wasn't prepared for the intense competition emerging in our field. We didn't want to end up like the American steel or automobile industries.

Merck management had, I knew, a tremendous advantage over the workers. It didn't result from the conservative political environment fostered by the Reagan Administration, nor was it a product of the company's resources. Rather, it was a consequence of changes made at Rahway and elsewhere in the 1970s, when Merck had introduced automation and computer controls in all of its chemical and pharmaceutical plants. The same thing was happening throughout the nation's chemical businesses and oil refineries, most of which could now be operated by a few individuals standing in front of a control board.

Managers could run the plants, and that's what happened at Merck in 1984. All of the managers went on extended duty, and we were able to keep supplying pharmaceuticals to our customers from May through September without our unionized labor force. Since I didn't know how to run a control board, I put on an apron and took charge of the sandwich line in the cafeteria. I knew everything there was to know about making a sandwich.

As the strike finally ground to an end, Merck had to choose between becoming a nonunion operation or simply negotiating an agreement that would enable us to compete effectively. I didn't want Merck to break the union, so I was pleased when the company signed a conciliatory contract. The new agreement allowed Merck to bring labor costs back into line with those of its competitors and to regain some of the flexibility in work rules that we'd lost over the years.

\* \* \*

With the settlement completed, I quickly slid into a normal EVP schedule, which involved a great deal of travel. Diana made a couple of trips with me, but most of the time she was busy at our home in Watchung, New Jersey, with her own schedule and the family.

Meanwhile, I became familiar with the lounge at Newark Airport. Merck had plants in twenty-six countries, and I was determined to visit as many as possible. There's no substitute for face-to-face meetings. Absentee landlords don't do well in this business and perhaps not in any business. For one thing, the people running a plant in Ireland or Spain wanted to know that executives from headquarters are interested in what they've achieved.

I prepped very carefully for all these visits. Frank Spiegel had done a good job teaching me what all the numbers meant, and now I honed those new skills, digging in and figuring out what kind of performance I was evaluating. When I visited, I used every minute to get a better grasp of what the plants were accomplishing and what might be improved. Elaborate social events didn't interest me, although I had to take in the usual round of luncheons and dinners. I was more interested in one-on-one discussions, and I usually started my questions on the way in from the airport: "What do you see as your biggest problem in running the plant? Who are your best people? Are you getting support from Rahway?"

I was enjoying myself. I always learned something, and I was often able to make useful suggestions. On a visit to France, for instance, I discovered that we were making two kinds of *Primaxin*, our new antibiotic. "Why?" I asked. "Isn't the *Primaxin* the same?" "Yes," they explained, but the vials for Japan didn't have any particles in the solution. "Japanese physicians are finicky," they said, "and so you can't have any particles in the solution or they won't accept it."

After I exploded, I made an on-the-spot executive decision. "Look guys," I said, "if we're able to make a batch that's clear of particles, and that's our standard for Japan, we're going to use that as Merck's world standard!" They were stunned. Why take on extra refinements when they weren't required? I understood their reasoning, but I was determined that Merck be a tough worldwide competitor, now and in the future. Japanese firms were beginning to go global. In the long haul, they were likely to have a competitive advantage if their formulations were clearer than ours. Distributing an inferior formulation, even one that met FDA specifications, made no sense at all.

That may seem trivial, but I wanted everyone at Merck always to be concerned about our competitive position in matters large and small. I wanted the plants to improve their quality every year. Instead of hitting the standard and then focusing exclusively on cost cutting, I wanted them to lower costs through process improvements at the same time that they were upgrading quality. That made them sweat a bit. But in the long run, they too were pleased with the results.

The visits could have been painful for the local managers if they weren't so happy to see an interested executive coming from Rahway. To them, corporate headquarters often seemed a million miles away, populated by "suits" from another planet. As I tried to correct that view, I gathered hundreds of ideas about what I might do if I became John Horan's successor.

\* \* \*

After reviewing Merck facilities around the United States and the world, I could see that some things we had already established in the labs could be generalized across the entire company. We should, I thought, give more attention to recruitment to get better people in key positions. We weren't making phone calls to get suggestions from leading people in the various fields. We weren't being really tough about schools, recommendations, and records. I thought we could do better and was happy to say so. I wanted to upgrade personnel in every job, from bottom to top. It was just as hard to get managers to accept this as it had been in MRL. It's a lot of hard work. It takes time. But it's absolutely crucial if you want the best organization. Not just a good organization – the best.

My first year as executive vice president was also my last. On the brink of retirement, John Horan called in each of his four senior executives and asked each of us the same question: "Who should lead the company when I retire?" In effect, I recommended myself without making a recommendation. "John," I said, "I don't really care who's chosen to lead this company. If I don't get the job, I'll become CEO of some other pharmaceutical firm." I knew what was in the Merck pipeline and what I'd done to put it there. So did the analysts who covered our industry. I figured if John Horan and the Board didn't understand what was going on, I wasn't going to argue my case or worry about the decision.

The Board of Directors knew me by this time, so they didn't even bother to interview me. I never found out what they said about the succession and never asked. All I know is that John Horan called me into his office for a chat. "Do you want to be CEO?" he asked. I answered, "Thanks. When do I start?"

# CHAPTER SIX

# Winning in Global Competition

I'D LIKE TO TELL YOU THAT AS SOON AS I BECAME CEO AT Merck (on July 1, 1985), I cut a big deal and won the heavyweight business crown. But I didn't. I'd barely settled into my new office when I made my first mistake, a global whopper. It was just what you might expect from a green CEO who didn't want to acknowledge that his organization wasn't ready to slug it out, toe-to-toe, with a tough international competitor. The details, round by round, blow by blow, are engraved on my memory, but I'll try to gloss over the minutiae.

It was my first deal. ICI, the giant British chemical company, had approached Merck because they needed a modern cardiovascular drug to boost their sagging product line and were focusing on the ACE inhibitors.[1] Merck had an excellent candidate coming along in the clinic, lisinopril, our follow-on therapy to *Vasotec*. Our early clinical results were very positive. Lisinopril reduced blood

---

[1] See Chapter 4, footnote 6 on the ACE inhibitors.

pressure, was a bit more potent than *Vasotec*, and appeared to have a slightly longer duration of action.

On the basis of these results and our experience in the field, we were confident that our new product would be a success. ICI agreed and proposed that we both market the drug worldwide at the same time, competing against each other and using different brand names for the same therapy.

In exchange for lisinopril, ICI offered one of their compounds, a drug designed to stop the long-term ravages of diabetes. Diabetics suffer from diseases of the nervous system and kidney, and from damage to the retina that can result in blindness. A compound that could prevent all three effects would be a major breakthrough.

The risk, however, was high. ICI had some interesting results from animal tests but no convincing evidence from human clinical trials. So, from our point of view, the offer involved trading a sure thing of modest commercial potential for a compound with huge potential but also high risk. The negotiations, which lasted for weeks, were intense. Corporate Licensing handled Merck's side of the deal while I stayed on the sidelines.

Merck wasn't working on diabetes, and our laboratories urged me to negotiate for the rights to develop and sell the ICI product. If the drug worked, they said, it would be used very widely. It would also give Merck a foothold in an important new therapeutic area where Merck research would be able to make some significant contributions in the future.

I agreed but wanted to be certain we displayed due diligence before signing an agreement. I said we should first look at what American Home Products was doing with another drug also directed against the effects of diabetes. After looking at their pre-clinical data, however, we decided the British firm had the more promising compound.

Then, I turned to our marketing group and asked if they could sell lisinopril when they already had a similar drug, *Vasotec*, on the market. It's not always easy to sell a follow-on, especially when the first product is doing very well. "Would you rather we trade away lisinopril?" I asked. The answer was decisive: "No, no no, don't sell it! We can handle both." They were confident. They could, they said, go head to head with ICI and beat them in the marketplace – while continuing to promote the growth of *Vasotec* sales.

I welcomed that assurance because ICI was turning up the heat in the negotiations. They were considering, they said, another company's cardiovascular drug. Our negotiating team wanted assurance from ICI that if their diabetes drug failed to make it, Merck would get access to another ICI product, but the British team rejected that stipulation.

As the tension mounted, I became directly involved. With my negotiating team huddled around me, I talked to the ICI representatives by phone. They were unwilling to talk about any other ICI products and wanted an answer from us soon. They were playing hardball, and I flinched. I wanted their potential breakthrough drug and was now convinced by our marketing people that we could beat them in marketing lisinopril.

We agreed on the original proposal, and both firms set out to market lisinopril. Our brand name was *Prinivil*. ICI named the drug *Zestril*, which was a clever choice because most older treatments for hypertension caused a loss of energy – the patients complained that the medicine took the zest out of lives.

Unfortunately, the Merck marketing teams also lacked zest. Our other drugs were booming, and they found it more difficult than anticipated to get enthusiastic about Merck's second blood pressure drug. ICI's marketing group, in contrast, saw *Zestril* as the hot product that could turn around their lethargic sales. They cut their price, put their entire operation behind *Zestril*, and took about 55 percent of the lisinopril market.

At that time, Merck was unwilling to shave even a penny on price. The marketing people told me, "It's a Merck product! We will never give on price!" Each of our marketing and sales groups tried a slightly different approach, but none worked particularly well. In France, for instance, we shifted all our support to *Prinivil*, letting *Vasotec* sales slide dramatically. The increases didn't equal the declines, so there too we found ourselves losing overall market share in our antihypertension line.

As I could see after the fact, ICI looked at the world differently. With its roots in the bulk chemical trade where price competition is a way of life, the British firm knew exactly what to do with the product. We didn't. We were especially vulnerable where the bulk buyers – governments, hospitals, consumer organizations – were large. We couldn't win a bidding war because Merck's *Prinivil* and ICI's *Zestril* were the same drug. Large buyers knew that and were unwilling to pay for the Merck name.

The results were not disastrous, but they were embarrassing both for Merck and for me personally. I was further embarrassed when the "breakthrough" diabetes compound for which we had traded failed in clinical tests. We never learned whether the theory behind the drug was wrong or whether the compound was simply not good enough to block the complications from diabetes.

Later, the fair-minded chairman at ICI agreed that the deal was unbalanced and that his company owed Merck a product candidate. But when I retired as CEO, nothing had come of that promise. The failure in clinical trials for a high-risk, high-potential product like the one ICI gave us was commonplace in pharmaceuticals.

That was not surprising. But it hurt to have our deal go sour so early in my career as CEO.

If I'd continued to make deals like that one, my tenure as CEO would have been abbreviated. But I survived and learned several lessons from the ICI deal. I learned not to flinch when the other side put on pressure. I learned not to underestimate the opposition. And I learned not to overestimate our capabilities in research, manufacturing, or marketing.

*　*　*

The ICI fiasco and other experiences convinced me that I had to pay substantial attention to pumping up our marketing and sales forces. We had to turn Merck's domestic and international marketing and sales organizations into more nimble innovators and convince them that they could sell a second product in a therapeutic field. Even if it wasn't a blockbuster, even if the differences between our new product and the first entry were only marginal, and even if our new drug was similar to one being sold by the competition, Merck had to be able to market our products effectively.

The trick would be to do this without making any changes that would cut into marketing's great strengths. Once a large group of people is committed to a sound idea like "fair balance," it is wise not to tamper with that aspect of the operation. Marketing was already expanding on the idea of communicating complete information by conducting symposia, impanelling medical researchers to focus the attention of clinicians on therapeutic areas in which Merck was involved and on specific Merck innovations. In addition, marketing was hosting regional or local dinner gatherings where physicians could meet with a research clinician, a decision leader in a particular field. I wanted all these programs to continue.

I started the upgrade with the hardest part: recruiting the best people. In effect, we repeated the process I had already started at the labs, answering the same questions and applying steady pressure in the same way. I insisted that we place more emphasis on a candidate's record than on an interview. I wanted to hire the best, not the most charming.

In the international division, we had a sticky problem with leadership. Many of our top people overseas were not nationals. However talented they were, they simply could not elicit the loyalty of their people or recruit top talent the way a compatriot could. I worried about this and their inability to interact with government bodies as effectively as a local citizen. I insisted on seeking out top national talent, developing our own people with internal promotions, to carry the flag for Merck. In time, strong nationals led all our overseas subsidiaries, and our performance in these markets improved.

We also tried other ways to improve our personnel. For example, each year all Merck supervisors evaluated their "direct reports," that is, everyone working directly for them. Since most Merck people did satisfactory work, most of the evaluations clumped around a "satisfactory" level. Many of the numerical "grades" were exactly the same. We announced that supervisors could no longer give the same score to two direct reports. We wanted some differentiation: Who was the best?

Groans could be heard throughout the land of Merck, but we stuck with the new approach because we were determined to get the best people in the global pharmaceutical industry working for us. Most important, we wanted to know which of our people were the best – at every level – so that their compensation reflected their quality and accomplishments.

We also reorganized the marketing activities, and I quickly became a devotee of restructuring, reorganizing, or reengineering – whatever they were calling it at that time. Every time we reorganized, we had a chance to move the best people to the top and gracefully clean out some of the deadwood. As this suggests, I continued to be more concerned about people and their day-today performance than I was about organizational charts.

In marketing we started by creating a headquarters task force to appraise what we were doing worldwide and to propose specific improvements. At the same time, we increased our marketing personnel about 25 percent while steadily upgrading our critically important training programs. These programs focused on the evolving market in each country because they differed enormously. In the United States, regulatory approval from the FDA allowed immediate launch of the product at a price set by the company. In many of our major foreign markets, launch of a new product required not only government regulatory approval but also government pricing approval – a process that sometimes took many additional months of negotiations. The task of educating physicians about our products also required different approaches in our varied national markets.

Overseas, we made a number of structural and personnel changes. Merck was logging double-digit growth in Europe, but I still thought we could improve those operations with more global centralization. This was not a risk-free change. Although centralization cuts costs and lets you develop global performance standards, it can dampen innovation. Furthermore, you can lose the support of local heads who resent the loss of autonomy. To reap the benefits and minimize the downsides, you have to manage the transition carefully and be sure to have effective leadership at the top and throughout middle management.

We started by restructuring or eliminating some subsidiaries in Latin America, Asia, and Africa that weren't performing up to our standards and kept fine tuning to find the right balance between centralization and decentralization. This process never ends, but by 1994 Merck was certainly a more focused, more centralized multinational better prepared for the intense global competition the industry would face in the next two decades.

\* \* \*

Managed care in the United States was one of the areas in which I thought Merck was responding too slowly. It was obvious by the 1980s that the U.S. healthcare system had to change dramatically and that some form of managed care was the wave of the future. In 1988, about 30 million people were already enrolled in managed care, such as an HMO, and our studies indicated that many more Americans would soon join them. Merck had fallen behind in responding to this change in the market. Needing experts in negotiating contracts with large buyers, we created a new department fully dedicated to handling HMO accounts. We did the same thing for our hospital business.

After we got this reorganized marketing organization humming, we took the next giant step. In 1991 we created a single worldwide marketing organization, the Merck Human Health Division. Once again, organizational change enabled us to move promising executives with extensive experience in European marketing, toward the top. One of the least understood aspects of organizational change is the opportunity it provides to alter the business's leadership cadre.

The presidents of our European subsidiaries opposed this change, but they were on weak ground, defending national autonomy when all of Europe was rapidly consolidating. We, on the other hand, were moving with the flow of history, not against it. Where products had special marketing needs – in animal health and crop protection, specialty chemicals, and vaccines – we kept the operations in separate divisions. But the heart of our business, drug therapies for humans, was now gathered into one marketing organization with unified high standards for manufacturing, marketing, and sales around the globe. This way, we could be even more confident of the quality of our products and the quality of the information transmitted to physicians in all of our markets.

We were still vulnerable on one major front. Pharmacy benefit management organizations (PBMs) were revolutionizing the way many Americans purchased our medicines. Labor unions, government organizations, such as the country's largest federal employee benefit program, and many big companies like General Motors provided prescription drug benefits to their employees, including retirees. All these institutions were struggling to hold down their soaring healthcare costs, and they were wisely contracting with the PBMs to provide prescription drugs to their members.

The PBMs controlled costs by high-volume purchasing and by developing more efficient means of delivery – including mail systems – than the corner drugstore. They drove hard bargains with pharmaceutical companies that wanted to place their products on the PBMs' formularies, their lists of acceptable medicines. They also cut the costs of treatment by ensuring that patients received generic drugs wherever possible. Using mechanized, computerized delivery systems, the best PBMs developed an enormous database with multiple benefits. They sharply cut the rate of errors in filling prescriptions while vastly improving the speed and efficiency with which orders were filled.

The PBMs could compare the costs to patients and providers of different therapies that had the same or very similar profiles. They could improve patient care because all prescription information, along with background data concerning the patient's potential adverse reactions, was maintained on the PBMs' computers and made available to a pharmacist whenever a plan member requested a new prescription.

The leading firm in the industry was Medco Containment Services, Inc., which the entrepreneur Marty Wygod had pushed to the top of the business. Medco was particularly good at selling its services to large organizations, at shifting market share within a class of drugs to their preferred product, and at driving down costs. By 1992 Medco was serving 38 million people – an astonishing number for such a young enterprise.

Since Medco and the other PBMs were established in a strong position between Merck and its customers, I decided to consider integrating forward into that business. We formed a high-level task force that recommended acquiring the strongest of the PBMs, Medco. We put together a small team and launched negotiations with Wygod, who was already talking to Bristol-Myers Squibb and others about a possible acquisition. This sent us into high gear, and I stayed very close to these discussions. Medco was the most desirable acquisition of the PBMs, and the government was likely to approve it. Our first move was to set the right price for Wygod's creation.

Wygod had recognized an unusual business opportunity, built a powerful organization to capitalize on that opening, and created value for his customers and his company. Along the way, he had hired several intense, talented executives, who worked together extremely well as a team. Wygod's accomplishment was an outstanding example of what modern American entrepreneurship could accomplish. Now we had to calculate just how much value Wygod had created, and that was determined in a series of complex, multisided negotiations.

From the sidelines I stayed in close touch with my negotiating team, hoping the price would be $5 billion or less. But Wygod's price was $6.6 billion, and that's what we paid to stay ahead of the pack and close to our customers. Four decades after Merck had integrated into pharmaceuticals by acquiring Sharp & Dohme (1953), Merck led the U.S. industry into a new era of improved patient care and cost control.

The formation of Merck–Medco was a unique strategic move in response to the needs of Merck's customers – both individual consumers and employers that provided prescription drug benefits. It positioned the firm to communicate directly with millions of patients who could now acquire their drugs more easily, with more accuracy, and at lower cost. Indeed, by 1999, over 50 million persons were covered by Merck–Medco plans. One direct benefit of our acquiring Medco was that Merck drugs attained a higher market share within the Merck–Medco formulary than they had achieved in the broad U.S. market. This gave a strong boost to Merck sales in this country.

All of these experiments in marketing had a latent objective. We were looking for a way to replace the traditional sales reps with a new method of getting information to physicians. I wanted to reduce the sales force, which I considered an expensive, inefficient relic of the past. But in this case, I was an unsuccessful innovator. The experiment failed, in part because it had to be run through a sales force that had every reason to be suspicious of innovation along these lines.

Nevertheless, I remain certain to this day that the company that successfully changes the pharmaceutical sales-rep paradigm will revolutionize the industry. In this day of high-speed information technology, pressure on physician time, pressure on prices, and intense competition, someone will break this mold. My bet is that it will be broken by a small company with no sales force – a firm that has an important product and a smart, risk-taking CEO. Eventually, the big pharmaceutical companies will follow the leader, but in the meantime they will be stuck with the huge, antiquated sales forces they are all continuing to enlarge.

* * *

I also had some ideas about how to improve our manufacturing operations. Here, as in marketing, Merck had some well-established strengths, including a number of accomplished people with the kind of technical training I considered a big advantage for those who wanted to get to the top in pharmaceuticals. Merck was particularly adept at moving new products from the laboratory into the factory.

Some of the credit for that goes to Dr. Max Tishler, one of my predecessors as president of the labs. Max was a first-class organic chemist who delighted in leaving the lab and mingling with the people working at the pilot plant and the factory. He was a high-energy driver who made his business his life and made Merck's research and development organization one of the best in the industry. Probably *the* best. By maintaining close, intense coordination between research, development, and manufacturing, Merck made the process of bringing new drugs to market far more efficient. I was now satisfied that we were systematically upgrading the quality of our chemical engineering.

But once we started to produce a new product like *Mevacor* or *Vasotec*, our manufacturing division seemed content to continue cranking out the drugs without making significant improvements annually in the production process. I thought we were missing opportunities to cut costs and improve quality through process innovations. I insisted on setting higher targets for improvements each year. Instead of raising prices, I wanted Merck to deal with inflation and achieve profit growth by increasing our share of the market.

Determined to strengthen our manufacturing capabilities, I became a preacher – and my sermons were not always appreciated. One of our experienced production men said I was too demanding. "Right after you win the Olympic high jump record," he said, "you don't want to be asked how high you're going to jump next time!" He was right: I always asked and kept pushing.

To complement the sermons, I looked for specific opportunities to foster major innovations in manufacturing. It was apparent to me that Merck's manufacturing operations had grown willy-nilly, driven by political necessity. When the company pushed into Latin America in the 1950s and 1960s, part of the price of entry had been agreements to manufacture as well as distribute pharmaceuticals in the various national markets. The same was true throughout much of Europe.

France was a particularly difficult country in which to grow our business. Negotiations there went through several stages. First you made a deal requiring you to establish a plant and start producing specific products. Then, in a separate deal, you had to negotiate the prices you could charge for your drugs. Finally, you had to sign an agreement saying you had done all this freely of your own will with no pressure from the government, which of course was not true.

Finally, in one case, in the last stage of the relationship, the French government cut the prices we had agreed upon in the negotiation that theoretically had never taken place. Even my sabbatical year in Paris had not prepared me for this style of doing business.

When it was apparent that *Vasotec* would be one of our biggest products, the French had asked us to produce all of the active ingredient, enalapril, for all of Europe in a new plant that we would have to build in France. Under our secret agreement, we would in return be allowed a decent price for the finished product. We built the plant, which made Merck one of the largest corporate taxpayers in France due to our huge quantity of exports within Europe. Soon after we were in full operation, however, the French government cut the price of *Vasotec*. Our executives in France protested to no avail. The government warned us not to take any precipitous action or we would be punished even further.

We waited, but they didn't reverse the price cut, and my patience finally ran out. We transferred our chemical operations to the United Kingdom and closed the French plant. Then we waited for a political explosion, but nothing happened. Our French subsidiary suffered no negative consequences and to the present day has continued to operate successfully. This experience taught me a bit more about negotiating and probably made me a little tougher when deciding how to reorganize our manufacturing.

When we reviewed the elaborate global production system we had created in this haphazard, ad hoc style, it was obvious we were unprepared for the long era of cost containment facing us and the rest of the industry in the 1980s and 1990s. Maybe even longer. We couldn't hold down costs if plants were not running at full capacity. We couldn't cut costs when we were producing the same chemical and pharmaceutical products in three, four, or five sites around the world.

Globalization was transforming the pharmaceutical business just as it was changing steel production, automobiles, and many other industries. A worldwide merger movement was just beginning to take place in these industries and ours, and one result of that transition would be, we thought, a long period of intense price competition. We had to be more efficient if we were going to be leaders in the global industry.

Recognizing that we needed to become competitive in every aspect of our business, we reorganized manufacturing in two stages. First, in 1989 we combined all of the company's pharmaceutical operations that produced our finished products in fourteen different countries under one division. The heads of the foreign subsidiaries screamed just as they had when we centralized marketing. They asked, "How can we deal effectively with our governments, the governments that in most cases set prices on all of our products, if we don't control pharmaceutical production?" They had a point, of course. But it was now more important to unify our operations and lower costs than it was to deal effectively with any single government. We were paying a short-term price to achieve a long-term gain in efficiency. Logic aside, our foreign heads were also angry over losing turf, and they made this transition painful.

Gradually, however, they came to appreciate that the new division lowered costs and accelerated the development of international standards in everything from environmental protection to production and marketing. Then, in 1991, we pushed the centralization one step further, pulling the bulk chemical production and the pharmaceutical manufacturing into one global organization that included thirty-one different plants.

Once more, restructuring enabled us to float another cadre of executives to the top. These were leaders with the combination of technical training and managerial ability that I favored. As a result, our productivity increases began to exceed the rate of inflation and provide a solid basis for growth in earnings.

These changes hurt some people, but many more would have been hurt much worse if we hadn't responded successfully to the new environment for healthcare in the United States and abroad. We tried to ease our employees through the transition with training programs and effective leadership, but we couldn't be in the business of subsidizing inefficient operations – a practice that can't be sustained over the long haul in a competitive setting.

\* \* \*

We didn't ignore R&D when we set out to improve our position as a global competitor. We were already satisfying a growing number of patients with new drugs like *Mevacor*, but it was evident to me that we could further broaden our drug development front. We steadily increased the annual budgets for the labs until, in 1994, we spent over $1.3 billion on research and development. Ed Scolnick built up our resources in molecular genetics and recombinant DNA technology, starting with specific projects like the one that produced the vaccine *Recombivax HB*. Soon Merck had a generalized capability in the new science and technology that we (and others) thought was the equal of any biotech company in the world.

Nevertheless, the breakthroughs were coming so fast and across such a broad front that we still found it useful to partner with small biotech companies having special skills. The combined opportunities for new drug development through molecular genetics, recombinant DNA technology, biochemistry and enzymology, crystallography, and medicinal chemistry were awesome. It was evident that even a billion-dollar R&D program couldn't cope with all the changes taking place in the biomedical sciences in the United States and abroad.

In my inner circle of advisers, we began intense discussions of what we could do to keep Merck at the front of the pack. One possibility was to increase the research budget by creating a much larger business through merger or acquisition. Since each of the world's major pharmaceutical firms tended to emphasize particular therapeutic categories, such as cardiovascular treatments or therapies for nervous disorders, a merger could have a quick impact on the new product pipeline if two firms with products in complementary therapeutic areas merged. Financial analysts watched these pipelines like birds of prey circling a potential meal.

Most of our successful competitors in the 1980s and 1990s pulled off at least one significant merger or acquisition. Some completed several deals and quickly built up their total sales. Bristol-Myers and Squibb merged, as did Hoechst and Marion Merrell Dow. American Home Products acquired American Cyanamid Company. After Glaxo acquired Burroughs-Welcome, the combined enterprises moved for a time into first place in total global revenue. Hoffmann-La Roche pushed decisively into biotechnology by acquiring Genentech. Despite this wave of combinations, the worldwide market for pharmaceuticals was still highly fragmented – a situation that seemed to me basically unstable. Further consolidation was, I thought, inevitable.

The momentum from within the industry and the financial markets was substantial, but we decided to chart a different course. We saw no advantage to acquiring a firm that was significantly less successful at new drug discovery and development than Merck. We had carefully observed what happened with Smith Kline, which had become a very successful company after Jim Black discovered

*Tagamet.* This was an astonishing breakthrough treatment for peptic ulcers, and it quickly became the largest-selling drug in the world. For a time, the leaders of Smith Kline were kings of the hill.

Intoxicated by success, they ignored the fact that their prominence was based on a discovery by one talented scientist working in a small British outpost of Smith Kline research. Jim Black left the company, just as he had earlier left ICI after inventing beta-blockers, a new treatment for hypertension. Without Black, the Smith Kline research laboratories were unproductive, as they had been for years before, and the money from *Tagamet* sales didn't change that situation. When *Tagamet* lost patent protection, Smith Kline was battered by generic competition and within a few years was a limping giant looking to be acquired.

Beecham took up that challenge, restructuring, and merging the operations to form SmithKline Beecham. But the long-term future of the combination still largely depended on the productivity of a research organization in need of change. It was not long before another merger followed: Glaxo Wellcome acquired the combine and formed Glaxo SmithKline.

These mergers were expensive. This was especially true given the high prices of pharmaceutical stocks during these years. It was also much more difficult to capitalize on a merger than most financial observers realized. The lengthy process of consolidating Merck with Sharp & Dohme offered useful lessons, some of which I had been forced to learn when heading our laboratories. It had taken decades and a great deal of managerial effort to stitch the seams between these two organizations. When that task was successfully completed, however, the combined enterprise was able to move to the forefront of the global industry – and that fact was always in my mind.

Late in my tenure as CEO, I seriously contemplated a merger. We discussed several possible partners – including Glaxo – but I thought there was only one competing firm in the entire industry really worth all the trouble and expense a merger would entail. That firm was Pfizer. Our product lines largely complemented each other, and I yearned to graft the research potential of Merck to the marketing power of Pfizer. But Merck was so successful on its own that I couldn't persuade my colleagues to pursue this combination. This initiative didn't get off the ground even though I thought it would have created the strongest pharmaceutical research organization in the world. Nor could I generate the necessary enthusiasm in Bill Steere, the recently promoted CEO of Pfizer. I backed off. It wasn't wise to push hard for this merger when, owing to my impending retirement, I wouldn't be able to help the combination succeed.

Instead of mergers, Merck negotiated a series of strategic alliances. One example was our joint venture with Johnson & Johnson, a company with a leading position in the over-the-counter business. We had products with great potential for over-the-counter sales. J&J had marketing capabilities for our over-the-counter products that would have cost us many millions of dollars and several years to develop. Even then, we might not have been successful in what for Merck was a new undertaking. By handling the over-the-counter business through a joint venture – Johnson & Johnson • Merck Consumer Pharmaceuticals Co. – both firms could maximize their existing strengths. We were winners, but so were the consumers and a national economy that needed powerhouse multinational competitors willing to explore new avenues to innovation.

That venture began when Jim Burke, CEO of J&J, and I met in Washington, DC, waiting to board a plane and return to New

Jersey after a Business Council meeting. Burke and I took advantage of our wait to talk about the over-the-counter potential of *Pepcid*, our prescription treatment for peptic ulcers. This product had been on the market several years, and we had a high degree of confidence in its safety. *Pepcid* had been, however, the third entry in the field of peptic ulcer medicines behind SmithKline Beecham's *Tagamet* and Glaxo's *Zantac*. Now our question was: Could a Merck–J&J venture get to the over-the-counter market first and achieve an advantage over these two strong competitors? On the spot, we decided we could and agreed to organize a team to bring our companies together. The race was on.

Our collaboration went smoothly. Merck research quickly developed the new over-the-counter formulation and received the FDA's approval. The J&J forces guided the new brand, *Pepcid AC*, onto the market ahead of our two competitors and promoted it with vigor and skill. We developed brand loyalty, which is as important to over-the-counter products as patents are to prescription drugs. *Pepcid AC* never lost its lead. Together, J&J and Merck increased the value of *Pepcid* enormously by taking it over-the-counter, and in fact the prescription version, owing to these marketing efforts, gained market share at the same time.

We continued down this path with other alliances. One was with DuPont, a company which had an innovative drug but needed Merck's established capabilities in development, regulatory affairs, marketing, and sales. We already had in place a joint venture with the Swedish firm Astra, and we were also able to establish mutually profitable links to Sigma Tau, a leading Italian company, and to Pasteur Mérieux Sérums & Vaccins in order to develop new combination vaccines for global markets.

Our strategic alliances and the improvements in manufacturing, marketing, and sales enabled us to take full advantage of the wave of new products emerging from the Merck Research Laboratories. I could, of course, simply have ridden that wave, enjoyed life, and looked forward to retirement with a nice package of Merck stock and a clear conscience. But that would have left the firm poorly positioned for the coming era of intense global competition. I wouldn't even contemplate a passive strategy. I wanted Merck to be able to exploit every opportunity opening up in the biomedical sciences, and I wanted everyone in the company to help achieve that goal. Literally, everyone.

\* \* \*

To maximize our opportunities for successful innovation – or even come close – we had to narrow our focus. Merck had dabbled with diversification, acquiring a specialty chemicals operation that made everything from granulated carbon to thickeners for salad dressing. In the years that followed our initial moves into diversification, each of these enterprises acquired a momentum of its own. They kept growing, innovating, and making profits, and so there was no good reason to disturb them.

When I became CEO, I was advised to consider further diversification. But I didn't think Merck needed to camouflage its profitability, and I didn't want management to spend time thinking about water coolers, activated carbon, or salad dressing. Merck leadership had little expertise in these businesses, most of which did not have a high-tech component, and as a result they had been left to make their own way. I was uncomfortable with this arrangement. I was convinced that we could be the best in pharmaceuticals, and if we couldn't, salad dressing wouldn't be our salvation – however profitable it was. I began looking for ways to spin off our diversified operations at decent prices.

The group running Calgon Carbon Corporation brought off a managerial, leveraged buyout, and shortly after the deal with us was done, their new company's major competitor went in the tank. They were left sitting on a gold mine. Personally, I was as happy for them as I was for Merck, which had sharpened its focus and deepened its commitment to its core business.

We continued to divest non-core businesses. Next we sold Calgon Water Management in 1993. Last to go were Kelco and a smaller operation, Calgon Vestal Laboratories. Kelco had become a world leader in manufacturing alginates and biogums, some of which were produced from seaweed harvested in California waters. In addition to thickening salad dressing, Kelco's products were used in everything from oil exploration to skin care. Although Kelco and the Calgon Vestal Laboratories, which specialized in wound dressings, were both successful niche players, they too were peripheral to our central strategic goal.

Both were sold because they couldn't help us be the most innovative and successful firm in the global pharmaceutical industry. To achieve that goal, we made plans to exit all of Merck's remaining nonpharmaceutical businesses. This job was not completed when I retired, but by that time we had already significantly restructured the business and established our strategy for the future.

\* \* \*

The more we concentrated on pharmaceuticals, the more pressure we put on the Merck Research Laboratories, where Ed Scolnick was running the show. As CEO, I made certain that Ed and MRL had all the resources they could use successfully. We increased the research budget by 13 percent during my first year, added 18 percent two years in a row, and provided an additional 12 percent in 1989. At that point, we were spending over $750 million a year on research and development, which enabled us to open the Neuroscience Research Centre in England (which later developed *Maxalt*, Merck's new migraine drug). MRL was also able to double the R&D program in Canada, where the labs later discovered *Singulair*, a break through treatment for asthma, and *Vioxx*, an osteoarthritis and analgesic product that offered certain unique benefits (by not causing ulcers and bleeding, for instance) but has recently launched a wave of concern about possible side effects in Cox-2 inhibitors.[2] MRL also completed a new $80 million John J. Horan Research Building at Rahway.

When I was head of MRL, the company had concentrated substantial resources on rolling out big winners, including *Vasotec*, *Primaxin*, *Mevacor*, *Recombivax HB* (the hepatitis B vaccine), and *Pepcid*, but the labs were also working furiously to have backup and second-generation drugs ready. This kind of work doesn't make banner headlines or win prizes, but it was crucial to Merck and any other firm in the industry with global aspirations. Drug development is so slow and expensive that this follow-up work must be under way long before the blockbuster drug hits the market.

As CEO, I was pleased with the way Merck Research Laboratories was making improvements on each of our drugs and learning through clinical trials exactly what each could do for patients. This may seem elementary, but I'd seen many pharmaceutical companies fail to do this systematically, and it was one of the things I'd worked hard to change when I was heading Merck's research.

Now, Merck was harvesting the fruits of that transition. Under Scolnick's direction, MRL established through extensive clinical

---

[2] In 2004 Merck voluntarily withdrew its Cox-2 inhibitor, *Vioxx*, from the market after clinical data indicated an increased risk of cardiovascular problems for patients who had used the drug for an extended period.

trials that *Vasotec* was an appropriate therapy for patients suffering from congestive heart failure as well as hypertension. By combining *Vasotec* with *Hydro Diuril*, an older medication now off patent, MRL produced *Vaseretic*, which enabled physicians to give patients a diuretic, an antihypertensive, and a treatment for congestive heart failure in one dose – a convenience for many people. Merck Research Laboratories won no headlines for meticulous attention to this aspect of drug development, but the aggregate impact on the company's bottom line was significant. By 1990 Merck had eighteen drugs with annual sales reaching or exceeding $100 million, and the list included *Vaseretic* as well as *Zocor*, our follow-up to *Mevacor*.

In the late 1980s and early 1990s, MRL also began to add significantly to our core group of blockbuster products. The stars included four cardiovasculars, one antiulcer drug, and *Primaxin*, our leading anti-infective. In 1988, we started our rollout of *Prinivil*, the new ACE inhibitor we had developed as a backup to *Vasotec*. The following year we brought out an acid pump inhibitor, *Prilosec*, which strengthened our position in the market for ulcer treatments. Virus and cell biology contributed to the new wave of products with a pediatric vaccine against Hib (*Haemophilus influenzae* type b), a major source of meningitis in children.

\* \* \*

If we summarize Merck's strategic plan and present it in the bullet form characteristic of business and business school presentations, this is what we get for the years 1985 through 1994:

- We were steadily improving our personnel throughout the organization.

- We were pumping more resources into research and development while adding substantial new capabilities in molecular biology and genetics.
- We were systematically following up on the development of each of our new products, whether they came out of MRL or were licensed from another firm.
- We were upgrading our marketing operations.
- We were cutting costs and improving quality in manufacturing.
- We were tightening our concentration on the core business: developing, manufacturing, and selling pharmaceuticals.
- We were increasing our capacity for breakthrough research and innovative marketing through strategic alliances.

This kind of strategy made sense to me. It was entirely different from compiling projections from the different divisions and departments. The new Merck plan challenged every division and demanded innovation from every individual.

The industry was changing with hurricane force in the 1980s and 1990s, but by successfully implementing our strategy, we were able to keep Merck growing vigorously and producing the kind of profits that attracted the attention of Wall Street and Main Street. Between 1985 and 1993, we increased the company's total sales from $3.5 billion to $10.5 billion.

Our growth in Europe, where we were the leading U.S.-based competitor, was in double digits. Net income almost quadrupled, from $540 million to a little under $2.2 billion. When you add stock price appreciation to dividends to get the cumulative total stockholder return, we had created a compound annual growth rate of 24 percent during the ten-year period ending in December 1993. We were the largest pharmaceutical company in the world

Merck & Co., Inc. 1985–1994

| | Earnings/share | Stock high | Stock low | Annual sales (in millions) | Profits after tax (in millions) | R&D expenditures (in millions) | Number of employees |
|---|---|---|---|---|---|---|---|
| 1985 | $0.42 | 22.96 | 15.05 | $3,547.50 | 539.90 | 426.30 | 30,900 |
| 1986 | $0.54 | 43.17 | 22.38 | $4,128.90 | 675.70 | 479.80 | 30,700 |
| 1987 | $0.74 | 74.33 | 40.67 | $5,061.30 | 906.40 | 565.70 | 31,100 |
| 1988 | $1.02 | 59.63 | 48 | $5,939.50 | 1,206.80 | 668.80 | 32,000 |
| 1989 | $1.26 | 80.75 | 56.25 | $6,550.50 | 1,495.40 | 750.50 | 34,400 |
| 1990 | $1.52 | 91.13 | 67 | $7,671.50 | 1,781.20 | 854.00 | 36,900 |
| 1991 | $1.83 | 167 | 82 | $8,602.70 | 2,121.70 | 987.80 | 37,700 |
| 1992 | $2.12 | 56.63 | 40.5* | $9,662.50 | 2,446.60 | 1,111.60 | 38,400 |
| 1993 | $1.87 | 44.17 | 28.63 | $10,498.20 | 2,166.20 | 1,172.80 | 47,100 |
| 1994 | $2.38 | 39.5 | 28.17 | $14,969.80 | 2,997.00 | 1,230.60 | 47,500 |

* Merck stock split 3/1, effective May 6, 1992. The common stock had previously been split 3/1, effective May 4, 1988.

and, in my opinion, the most successful innovator in an industry with a great track record for entrepreneurship.

It was a pleasure for all of us to contemplate these accomplishments when Merck & Co., Inc., celebrated its centennial in 1991. Given our dedication to change and our acknowledgment that everyone in the company, from bottom to top, had contributed to our success, we granted stock options (100 shares) to all 34,500 of our employees throughout the world. For some years, I had been looking for a way to make everyone an owner as well as a worker. The centennial gave me the opening I needed to give everyone at Merck a chance to acquire an owner's stake in our future.

# CHAPTER SEVEN

# Prices and the Public Interest

O NE OF THE MOST DIFFICULT ISSUES I STRUGGLED WITH during my tenure as CEO involved the prices of our products. Pricing of pharmaceuticals will always be a thorny issue because drugs and vaccines are literally matters of life or death for many people. When a physician prescribes a particular medication, the patient seldom has a choice about which one to buy. The physician has already made that choice. Health insurance, a health maintenance organization, or Medicare is likely to pay the physician's bill but many of the plans did not pay for prescriptions, which were, and still are, relatively expensive. If patients are not covered by a plan that provides low-cost prescription drugs, the pain of payment is immediate and memorable.

As a physician who grew up during the Great Depression, I understood their distress, and as CEO at Merck I became very concerned about our pricing policy. At first, I didn't really understand the nitty-gritty of what was going on in the marketplace. When things are going well, the CEO doesn't press the managers very much. He wants to give them freedom to do what they do.

But I was fretting about prices, and so I started a dialogue within the firm about this issue.

In general, Merck priced according to the value that its products contributed. If our new drugs made a substantial difference in treatment of a disease compared with earlier products, our price was going to be higher. We knew that many of our medicines, even when they were expensive, kept people alive, reduced overall healthcare costs, and kept people on the job. They also improved the quality of life. We tried to set the price so that a majority of the potential users would be able to afford the drugs, but we also never lost sight of the fact that our research and development costs were steadily increasing and that sustained innovation by the laboratories was the key to Merck's success. In effect, we were trying to achieve a successful balance between public good and private gain.

Once we had set what we considered to be a fair price for a product, we had to deal with the issue of annual price increases. Here, I had a different view than most of my marketing executives and certainly the rest of the industry. I wanted to keep increases low because I wanted to continue to get medicines into the hands of people who needed them, many of whom were clearly distressed about the prices they were paying for their prescriptions.

When I pressed our marketing people about price increases, they had answers for all but one of my questions. Their story went like this: "We had a long period of severe inflation in the 1970s, when costs went up faster than we could increase prices. Our margins got tighter and we weren't certain we could pay for our expensive R&D if that continued indefinitely." Because I'd headed MRL when that was happening, they thought I would be susceptible to that argument. I was. But not enough to let this matter slide off the table. I continued to worry about whether we still needed to raise prices to make up for an "inflationary gap" that had developed long before I was CEO.

I began to watch the statistics on prices very carefully. I kept pressing – in part because I thought the gap had disappeared and in part because it seemed that we were frequently making up for our failure to increase the volume of our sales by increasing our prices. We weren't doing that with vaccines because there volume was increasing and prices were more stable, partly as a result of large-volume government purchases.

In fact, prices for vaccines were too low and were driving competitors out of the business. At one point, I stunned the management group by suggesting the price for a hepatitis B vaccine could be $100 per person (three shots were required). The marketing group reacted as though I were crazy at the time, but the price they came up with several years later when we had the vaccine was $100 per person. We could stay in the business at that price – especially after the liability problem for childhood vaccines was largely solved by a new law (prompted by Merck and others) that added a tax to each vaccine proportional to the incidence and importance of the side effects. Children who had side effects could receive compensation without resort to courts. This law and our new approach to pricing permitted Merck and a few others to continue to invest long term in this important field.

But we were increasing the prices of prescription drugs faster than I thought we should. It was one thing to charge a relatively high price on a breakthrough drug like *Mevacor*. Patients were paying for value delivered by a new therapy that didn't exist before. And, of course, a drug like *Mevacor* initially faced very little competition. It was another thing to raise prices with mature products still covered by patents.

In fact, however, we could raise prices and increase total revenue even on products facing generic competition because many physicians prescribed our branded drugs long after generics were on the market. Some doctors were just doing what they had done for years without thinking about the economic consequences for their patients. Others were confident about the quality of Merck's products and somewhat suspicious of generics. Whatever the reasoning, many physicians were behaving just as our marketing experts said they would and, without knowing it, sustaining the pricing policies that were causing me concern.

In the late 1980s, my anxiety about pricing intensified. By that time, the "inflationary gap" had been closed by annual price increases. When I talked to people outside of Merck, people in my local community and elsewhere, I heard a great deal about the trouble they were having paying for prescription drugs. I could see a wave of discontent building up in the American public.

I wasn't the only one to react to these tremors of concern. The media hyped the subject, focused and personalized the concerns, and began to offer specific suggestions about how to solve what was now identified as a national problem. That quickly brought the politicians into play, and they too began to develop ideas about measures that would appeal to the public and have some chance of being implemented by Congress. This is the normal stuff of democratic politics. When the process works properly, our national and state governments solve problems on a regular basis. That is, they respond to new situations by changing our laws and regulatory systems. Of course, the solutions always take longer than we want and entail compromises. As Winston Churchill explained, "Democracy is the worst form of government, except all those other forms that have been tried from time to time."

But even in a democracy, a great danger lies in implementing short-term solutions that have unintended consequences over the long term. That's especially likely to happen when problems are multifaceted or have vague origins. There was nothing vague about people's concerns over the prices of prescription drugs. People without drug benefits from insurance plans had quite specific stories to tell usually involving a huge bill that they paid regularly to refill a prescription. Often, they knew exactly how much each pill cost. But this issue was often mixed in people's minds with another, related national problem involving the large number of Americans not covered by any kind of medical insurance.

This was – and still is – a national scandal. Many of these people were forced to go to emergency wards when they were ill, which is an incredibly inefficient way to deliver healthcare. Individuals who have to sit for hours in the emergency ward do not get the kind of personal attention they would receive from a regular family practitioner. Furthermore, this situation stresses the capabilities of the emergency wards and the resources of the municipalities that support them. Without insurance and without money, people can't go regularly to a doctor, and instead of a $15 co-pay charge for medicine, they are faced with a $60 or even a $90 bill for their prescription drugs.

What would we do, I asked our marketing folks, if this volatile situation resulted in price controls? That was the question for which they had no answer. The price control policies in Europe had already cut deeply into the ability of European firms to innovate. Two-thirds of the pharmaceutical innovations were coming out of the United States, where markets still had a major influence on prices.

Recognizing that these two issues – increased prices and the threat of price controls – were being joined in the public mind and that Merck and the rest of the industry were drifting into a dangerous situation, I finally forced the issue and developed a new approach to pricing. As far as possible, I wanted to encourage all the other pharmaceutical firms to follow our lead without breaking the antitrust laws. I never discussed prices with any Merck competitor. From time to time, other CEOs delicately introduced the subject of prices, but I always quickly changed the subject. Talking prices was a quick way to get into deep trouble, and besides, our strategy was to succeed by continuing to be the industry's premier innovator.

In 1990, I proposed that Merck change its entire approach to pricing pharmaceuticals. Since at that time Merck was the market leader in the United States, I thought we had a good opportunity to make our policy the industry standard. From now on, I said to our top executives, we should unilaterally adopt a policy of not raising our prices any faster than the increases in the Consumer Price Index (CPI). That didn't go down well with our marketing experts. "You're leaving money on the table," they cried. They repeated this several times because they were absolutely convinced they were right. Actually, I knew they were right.

The marketers were deeply concerned about attaining revenue growth, a measure of their success each year. I was too, but I was also deeply concerned about the health of the research organizations in our firm and the rest of the industry. If we adopted this pricing policy, we would certainly be leaving money in the pockets of the people who bought our products. But if we didn't do this, I maintained, we were headed toward a major political crisis.

After a series of memorably intense discussions, we decided to adopt the new standard and to use an average figure for any increase in our prices. We took into account all of our products and keyed the increase to the CPI. Using an average figure was a compromise that gave marketing a little flexibility and served to stop most of the grumbling within the company. But once we announced our new policy, a burst of grumbling arose from outside Merck. Although some of our competitors quickly adopted our new standard, others were angry with Merck and with me personally.

Then, slowly, even the companies that were kicking and screaming followed the leader – probably for fear of being subjected to intense criticism. In time Merck's policy became the entire industry's policy, and we avoided the creation of a new government bureaucracy to control prices. At that point, we had clearly signaled our willingness to cooperate in solving the country's healthcare problems.

* * *

We employed a somewhat similar logic in dealing with vaccine issues. These too were very thorny political problems, in part because many of our vaccines protect children and in part because the pricing and delivery issues were so poorly understood. Even some of our nation's brightest political leaders seemed to be unwilling or unable to get a solid grip on these issues.

The vaccine crisis of those years was of vital importance because the best way for any society to deal with infection is to prevent it. The immunization of large populations against disease is extraordinarily efficient and cost-effective. But during the 1970s, several major U.S. vaccine manufacturers left the business. Part of the problem was liability. Vaccines are administered to healthy people, but there's always a small, relatively predictable number of side effects for each shot. These side effects are especially devastating when they involve children. Executives at several companies decided they were unwilling to deal with those problems since the profit margins on vaccines were very tight. It was simply more profitable to invest in new drugs than in new vaccines.

Merck, which had an outstanding vaccine program, had also seriously reconsidered its investments in this program when I was still heading the laboratories. The Merck operation was spearheaded by Dr. Maurice Hilleman. Hilleman was a world-famous virologist who had developed every vaccine Merck was producing, including a measles–mumps–rubella combination used throughout the United States and many other countries. Maurice ran the entire vaccine program, from laboratory through production line. He ran this operation in a meticulous, albeit dictatorial fashion, along the way cowing some company employees, including a few who were, theoretically, his superiors.

In the late 1970s, after many years of struggling to develop a vaccine against hepatitis B, Maurice and his troops were at last successful. Merck's breakthrough vaccine was produced from a particle that could be recovered from the plasma of persons infected with hepatitis B. I thought it was phenomenal that we would soon have a vaccine against a disease that was a leading cause of death in many Asian and African countries. The disease often progresses into cirrhosis or liver cancer, which kills as many as a quarter of those who are chronically infected. In China, where 13 percent of its massive population consisted of infected "carriers," hepatitis B was the nation's number one public health problem.

Knowing this and having closely followed Maurice's progress, I was upset when a Merck planning team produced a report that was highly critical of the economics of our vaccine program. I couldn't argue with the figures, which were correct. One curve showed the total revenue from vaccine sales and another the costs of Hilleman's vigorous research program. The two lines were drawing together ominously for the future of Merck vaccines. It was numbers like these that had persuaded several of our U.S. competitors to leave the business.

When the management committee met to discuss the report, I was nevertheless determined to shoot it down. Merck, I insisted, was different from the companies retreating from the vaccine business. Merck had a well-deserved reputation for social responsibility. It was *the* major American vaccine innovator and producer, and it had a powerful obligation to carry forward in that role and to try to make the business profitable. "Preventive medicine is the best medicine," I said. "That's what Merck should be making."

I was taking a long-term perspective shaped in large part by concern for the healthcare implications of the decision. Would a business school graduate have reached a different conclusion? Many in pharmaceutical firms in the United States seem to have done so, leaving the country with a sharply reduced capacity for innovation and production of vaccines. I was, however, absolutely certain my position was best in the long run, both for Merck and for society. Fortunately John Horan, who was CEO at that time, agreed, and Merck decided to stay the course.

The outlook on vaccines nevertheless turned even gloomier when events none of us had anticipated combined to undermine Maurice's *Heptavax-B*. Just as Merck was bringing out America's first hepatitis B vaccine, the AIDS pandemic hit the United States. At first no one understood the new disease, but doctors and patients quickly became suspicious of any plasma-based vaccine. In the case of *Heptavax-B*, the plasma had to be obtained from persons chronically infected with hepatitis B, many of whom were gay or intravenous drug users. These were the two major high-risk groups in the U.S. population identified with the HIV infections that led to AIDS – and, at that time, almost certain death. Our purification methods ensured that there were no live viruses of any kind in the vaccine, which the FDA had confirmed. However, so little was known at the time about HIV/AIDS, and the fear surrounding it was so pervasive, that no amount of scientific evidence could convince people to take a vaccine that had even the slightest possibility of containing an agent that caused the deadly infection.

This left us standing at a significant crossroads. Since Hilleman was approaching retirement at that time, it would have been relatively easy just to let his *Heptavax-B* vaccine dwindle – and with it our entire vaccine program. But I had supported our program in vaccines before, and now that I was the company's CEO, I wasn't going to give up. The reasons for continuing seemed to me just as powerful as they had been earlier.

What I decided to do, even before the AIDS crisis hit, was to march forward, but up a different scientific path. To that point, every viral vaccine had been made from either a killed or attenuated virus. I thought we might use a new approach, recombinant DNA (rDNA) technology, to produce a vaccine that was effective and entirely safe because it would not contain any of the original virus. Since my sabbatical year in Paris, I'd been following with great interest the advances in molecular genetics. From what I knew about recombinant DNA technology, I suspected we might be able to insert the hepatitis B viral DNA into a safe, noninfectious organism. That organism, instead of the virus, would make the particle we needed. In effect, the new technology could turn cells such as *E. coli* into tiny factories.

The process wasn't going to be simple, of course, and so I had looked outside MRL for help. I knew Bill Rutter, an outstanding scientist at the University of California in San Francisco and one of the leading authorities on the new technology, and I decided to talk to him about Hilleman's vaccine. I explained to him that we were making *Heptavax-B* by isolating it from infected plasma. This was very dangerous for the plant workers who were isolating the antigen from the plasma, which contained live virus that could infect them.

Rutter agreed to try to get *E. coli* to produce, or "express," the surface antigen we needed. We set up a collaboration, with Merck's Jerry Birnbaum operating as the go-between. After considerable effort, Rutter and the *E. coli* appeared to be successful, but we soon discovered that the bacterium produced a form of the antigen that was slightly different from the natural substance. We had to change course again.

Now we turned to Ben Hall, a leading yeast geneticist at the University of Washington in Seattle. He and Bill Rutter collaborated in a new effort to put the hepatitis B surface antigen gene into baker's yeast cells. Bill and Ben already knew each other, and so it was easy to get them going on a joint project. This time the yeast cells produced an active surface antigen that in turn evoked the kind of immunological response we needed to make a vaccine.

That was still a long way from having a successful product, but some years later, after an extended experience with intense process development, Merck was able to bring out the world's first recombinant DNA vaccine for humans, *Recombivax HB*. Leading that development was the man I had recruited to take my place at MRL, Ed Scolnick. Ed's success, which encouraged me to believe that MRL had the leadership it deserved, enabled us to save Merck's vaccine against hepatitis B.

*Recombivax HB* was an immediate shot in the arm, so to speak, for our vaccine program. At first, it was used only with people facing a high risk of contracting hepatitis B, but the group of recipients was gradually increased until eventually it included all children in the United States.

This vaccine also became important internationally. It laid the foundation for what in the next few years would become an expanded global program of vaccine research, production, and marketing. It had, for instance, a significant and lasting impact on Merck's relationships with the People's Republic of China and the Chinese government's public health program. I'll give you some details on that unanticipated result in the final chapter.

In the United States, the successful cooperation between Merck, Bill Rutter, and Ben Hall helped launch two biotech start-ups. Rutter and Hall both became wealthy entrepreneurs, and royalties from the sales of *Recombivax HB* were major sources of revenue for their start-up firms, Chiron and Zymogenetics, as well as the University of California, San Francisco, and the University of Washington in Seattle, where the early experiments with recombinant technology were carried out. Innovation tends in these ways to spill over and have positive results that never show up in the balance sheet of your firm. They are as important to society as they are to the business system.

\* \* \*

I wish all of my experiences with vaccines and pricing were as positive as the *Recombivax HB* story, but they weren't. In fact, both subjects were central to one of the worst experiences I had as a CEO. No mistake. It was my own fault that it happened.

It all began pleasantly, in September 1992, when Bill Clinton's presidential campaign asked if their candidate could deliver a major address at Merck's company headquarters in Rahway. After some probing, we learned that Clinton's team had targeted Merck for the candidate's first important speech on healthcare reform.

Why Merck? I thought they'd chosen our company in part because of its reputation within the pharmaceutical industry.

During the previous year, Merck had introduced its new pricing policy, keying increases to changes in the Consumer Price Index. That innovation had received a great deal of favorable press as had our earlier policy on *Mectizan*, the drug for people endangered by river blindness. Merck was riding high, enjoying the kind of public acclaim for which every business and every CEO yearns. The firm was an ideal platform for a major address on healthcare.

As CEO, I couldn't avoid involvement in politics, even though some of my previous forays into the field hadn't been very pleasant. The *Mectizan* project, for instance, had sent me visiting federal agencies and some top-level officers in the Reagan Administration, none of whom were as concerned about conquering river blindness as Merck was. I didn't give up easily. But another trip to Washington produced the same results. On other occasions, I'd been invited to break the rules on campaign contributions, so my encounters with party politics and many of our politicians had left me skeptical about the ethical dimensions of American politics.

But whether I liked it or not, I had to do what every other CEO has to do: swallow hard and get involved. That meant handling campaign contributions through political action committees and personal contributions – in my case, all strictly by the rules. It meant supporting lobbying groups to pressure the state and federal governments on significant public policies affecting our industry. You have to be personally active in politics. If you don't do these things, your business will suffer. I was active, even though I knew that it wasn't my strong suit.

So it was not without reason that I was cautious on that sunny September day when Clinton spoke in front of the original Merck administration building. Thousands of excited employees poured out to hear the talk. We knew very little about this particular candidate, but what little I knew seemed interesting. He was smart, well trained, had already been a governor, and had some new ideas about reforming healthcare in the United States. I was anxious to meet him. My initial response to the man was very positive. I thought, "Maybe I can really get behind this candidate and work to improve healthcare in this country."

I agreed with a number of things Clinton said that day. He mentioned some of the strengths of the U.S. system but noted that our pharmaceutical companies were investing too little in the discovery of important new drugs and too much in low-risk projects to develop drugs similar to existing products. The exception, he said, was Merck, which had invested heavily in research and contributed many breakthrough products. His reference to Merck was important to this crowd, standing right across the street from the labs that had given the world some of its most important new therapies.

Several of Clinton's remarks made me nervous, however. Some of his "except for Merck" remarks, obviously added just for this occasion, worried me. He talked about costs, noting that healthcare in the United States soaked up about 13 percent of our gross domestic product – the highest percentage among the major developed nations. He criticized the high prices charged by physicians, hospitals, and pharmaceutical companies, saying those prices had to be controlled.

This last point really worried me. Clinton made it clear that he was leaning toward government price controls. I was deeply concerned that Congress might create what would become a rigid set of bureaucratic controls that would inevitably corrode the research-intensive component of our pharmaceutical and biotech industries. It was no accident that the United States was producing such a high percentage of the basic pharmaceutical innovations in the entire world. This country had created a remarkable combination of government, nonprofit, and private organizations, all of which were involved in an exciting, effective search for new therapies and preventive medicines, including vaccines.

Other countries, even those with superb scientific establishments, had fallen behind the pharmaceutical industry in the United States. In many cases, foreign manufacturers had to contend with price controls, government purchasing of drugs, and other regulations that severely limited their ability to earn the profits that sustain large-scale, modern research laboratories. In other cases, political hostility to the use of recombinant DNA technology and research in genetics created an environment hostile to scientific progress. In some countries, the links between university research and industrial R&D were much less fruitful than they were in America.

Innovation in this industry was a complex, cooperative undertaking. Merck repeatedly turned to academic scientists, as it had to me some years before, seeking advice, assistance, and sometimes leadership. Understanding that, it was impossible to ignore the significant role the U.S. government played in drug discovery. After all, the great majority of our fundamental research was sponsored by the National Institutes of Health and the National Science Foundation and carried out at universities.

But anyone who knew anything about medical research knew that this basic research was transformed into effective therapies that improved human lives primarily in pharmaceutical company research labs. As CEO of Merck, it was impossible for me to accept a new system of political economy that would threaten the pharmaceutical industry's ability to remain an effective partner in the process of medical innovation.

After Clinton's speech, he and I talked privately for about an hour. "I want your advice," he said earnestly, looking directly into my eyes. "I really appreciate what you've done with your research and your pricing policy, and if I'm elected, I'll want you to come in and advise me." I was wary, given the tone and message of his speech. One slip, I thought, and Merck might no longer be called the exception to the rule. But I was impressed with his openness, his willingness to reach out for information, and his very warm, charismatic style. He had clearly demonstrated to his Merck audience what an effective politician he was. I agreed with many of Clinton's objectives, and I wanted him to have the chance to solve some of the country's healthcare problems. This was a relaxed, serious exchange of ideas. I was convinced that Clinton would take a partnership approach to reform. I was hopeful, earnest, and politically naive.

Shortly after being elected, Clinton held an Economic Summit in Little Rock. The stated objective was to formulate policies for the incoming administration, but even to a politically naive participant it was obvious that the Clinton team also wanted to drum up support for some reforms they had already pretty much defined. Attending one of the sessions, I found myself sitting at the round table directly opposite the President Elect. Clinton was the master of this situation, demonstrating the kind of political skill that had helped him win the election. He was agile and smooth and seemed open to advice. He was extremely comfortable with give-and-take on hot political issues.

During my turn at bat, he pointed out the importance of vaccines in preventing disease. He asked my opinion about vaccination of children in the United States. "Prevention of disease by vaccination," I said, "is the most efficient way to improve health." I described the progress Merck research had made in developing new vaccines. This had taken many years, I said, and had cost many millions of dollars.

Our exchange was friendly, even informative. I left the conference quite excited. "Bill Clinton," I said to myself, "is truly interested in improving healthcare and he's going to give it a high priority in his administration. He's smart enough to understand the issues and he's eager to get going."

A month later, I learned just how eager he was to "get going." The President blindsided Merck – and me personally – by attacking us for charging such high prices for our vaccines that American parents couldn't afford to get their children the shots they needed. Clinton came out blasting the industry. Our prices, he said, were "shocking." America's current situation was "unconscionable." The President warned: "We are running the risk of new epidemics spreading out in this country."

The President's blunt accusation was wrong, but that kind of political rhetoric appealed to many people. Even though the idea was false, it grabbed headlines and was quickly endorsed by the *New York Times*. What a sorry mess, I thought. We weren't going to solve America's healthcare problems with divisive political slogans that vilified companies like Merck, which was investing heavily in the development of new vaccines. If we were going to solve serious problems, we needed a partnership, not a political slugfest.

Both the President and the First Lady continued, however, to speak with compelling passion on this issue. They were deeply concerned, they said, because American children, especially those living in inner cities, were tragically undervaccinated. Both apparently believed that vaccination rates were low because our prices were high, as did Donna Shalala, Clinton's Secretary of Health and Human Services. I knew they were wrong, but just in case, I went back to our vaccine experts and got up-to-date information. As they explained, the worst problems were in urban centers where people relied heavily on hospital emergency rooms and clinics for their everyday healthcare. The clinics all used vaccines purchased by the government at about half the market price, and clinic physicians and nurses gave the shots to the children free. Price was not an issue.

Nevertheless, many parents didn't take their children for the free vaccines until they reached school age and the vaccinations were required for entry into school. Virtually all inner-city children get their shots by age four or five. The heart of the problem is children under age two. They are susceptible to diseases preventable by vaccination, but too many of them aren't getting their shots.

Why do parents wait? Some just don't get their acts together, but most find it hard to get to a clinic because of their jobs. They can't afford to sit for hours waiting for the shots. It seemed evident to us even back then that the United States needed new ways to help clinics, health maintenance organizations, emergency wards, and private physicians vaccinate preschool children. Something had to be changed.

We knew the problem wasn't Merck or the three other companies that supply most of the world's vaccines. I visited several Democratic leaders (including Ted Kennedy, Bill Bradley, Dan Rostenkowski, John Dingle, Frank Lautenberg, and George Mitchell) to explain this situation. I told them we wanted the federal government to put its money where it would do the most good. What America needed was a better tracking and distribution system for vaccines to ensure that more people would be vaccinated. Merck was already helping by providing support for local programs focused on this aspect of the problem. But increasing the supply of free vaccines was not the answer. "In some urban centers where too few children are being vaccinated," I said, "there is enough free vaccine to vaccinate every child *twice*!" All the politicians I contacted seemed to understand. But as Bob Rubin said to me in a moment of candor, "What the President wants to do is bad national policy, but he *is* the President and that's what he wants to do."

Indeed, Clinton did exactly what he wanted to do. It was virtually impossible for a politician to oppose anything that promised to help children, and the Administration's vaccine program sailed through Congress on the winds of political rhetoric. The Vaccines for Children program pumped more federal money into a system that badly needed an improved infrastructure, not cheaper vaccines. Before long, even the government began to recognize that the plan was based on false assumptions. The Government Accounting Office, which evaluated the Clinton policy, concluded that the price of vaccines was not preventing children from getting their shots. As the GAO discovered, neither the Clinton rhetoric nor the goal of increasing the supply of free vaccines was justified.

By that time, however, we had been badly bruised. The media and Washington both identified Merck and the other vaccine producers as opponents of reform. Actually, we were proponents of a new program to make vaccination more accessible to inner-city children at an early age. Merck also favored expanding healthcare insurance coverage, improving the quality of care, and limiting liability and bureaucracy, which were all changes that would allocate U.S. healthcare dollars more efficiently.

But that message didn't get through. I tried several times to act on the President's general invitation to "come in and advise me," but his office was never able to schedule a private meeting to talk about either vaccines or the general issue of healthcare reform. I saw him from time to time at fundraisers and other large occasions, and he continued to be extremely cordial. "Roy," he would say, "I really want you to come and visit."

\* \* \*

But the next Clinton with whom I consulted privately was his wife, Hillary Clinton. We had tea and talk at the White House. That conversation was my second eye-opener. We talked about the Administration's proposition to restructure the nation's entire healthcare system. This was a typical gathering of its kind. The First Lady brought her entourage, and I brought along four Merck people. Hillary sat on my left so we could address each other directly. She briefly summarized the President's plan, which we already understood very well – a series of new government organizations that seemed headed to thoroughgoing price control.

Then I summarized our plan: I wanted to see broader coverage by insurance and better management but with control left in the hands of the industry. Our team talked for about an hour. I emphasized the savings to individuals and the nation as a whole if we had a vaccination program that reached all children. We could take vaccines into the neighborhoods with mobile clinics or work through existing clinics and schools. I discussed the dramatic improvements in health produced by the combination of government and industry investment in biomedical research. I concluded, "It's our hope that all Americans can benefit from the fruits of this productive, cooperative enterprise."

At the end of our presentation, Hillary said, "Well, Dr. Vagelos, do you think you can support the President's plan?" I was stunned. "Of course not," I replied. "I just told you that we can't support the plan because it's very different from what I think would be best for the country." She quickly countered with a suggestion: "In that case, you could be neutral."

Again, I was surprised. I thought I had made myself clear. "What do you mean by being neutral?" I asked. "You just will say nothing," she replied.

"No, I can't be neutral because I head the largest pharmaceutical company in the world and we have a position which I represent. I will talk about it to the media and others if asked."

She then slammed the door on our talk: "Well, if you can't be supportive and you can't be neutral, then you are an enemy and you won't have any input."

The door that the First Lady slammed would not be opened to me during the remainder of the Clinton tenure. But she was wrong about my being an "enemy." I had spent my entire career – as a physician, a research scientist, a teacher of medical students, a research leader, and an executive in the pharmaceutical industry – trying to help patients in one way or another.

At Merck, we had been thinking about healthcare reform long before Bill Clinton was elected president. Our approach was incremental, and we explored reforms we thought would have a good chance of being implemented. We started with things we could do ourselves – first by limiting price increases and then by offering all Medicaid programs the lowest price we gave to any customer. Both these initiatives had ripple effects in the industry and the government that multiplied their impact.

Much more still had to be done. We wanted to balance universal access, individual choice, and continued innovation. That was a tall order, but we believed this could be achieved through "managed competition." I still think something along these lines could be implemented today. But there would have to be a dialogue more productive than that which I had with Hillary Clinton. In the end, the Clinton Plan created so many enemies that it went down in defeat. I hope the future will lead to creative compromises that change the current system as more and more Americans come to understand that our citizens' health needs to be protected as much as our national security.

*  *  *

The other pricing issue that came up was less politically charged but extremely important to both pharmaceutical customers and producers. This involved generics, a subject that has been in the international news lately. Even before I was CEO, we had every year or so been discussing the issue of generic versions of Merck products that went off patent protection. There was always a report that was presented by someone who looked to me like a smart high school student. I suspected the project was assigned to a very junior marketing person because the discussion was always short and always reached the same conclusion.

Once generic versions of a drug came on the market, the competition drove down prices. The generic producers had no significant R&D costs, they spent very little for the studies required for regulatory approval, and they did little promotion since they only emphasized prices. Merck's strategy had long been to avoid narrow-margin, commodity competition. Like "fair balance," this idea was deeply planted in the firm's sales and marketing mentality.

It wasn't planted in my mind, however, and so I asked them to explain why we couldn't manufacture generic versions of our own drugs. This irritated several of my marketing colleagues, but I persisted. "We've already got manufacturing plants producing the compounds. We must have already paid back the entire fixed cost of those plants. If we're at all efficient, we should be able to produce at a lower cost than any of our generic competitors."

"No, no!" came the replies. "You don't understand how this market operates." They explained that they didn't want to undercut the prices of our own branded products. Many physicians, having little incentive to change to generics, continued to prescribe Merck-branded products long after they had lost patent protection. "If we put our off-patent products under the Merck name," they said, "we'll shoot our own marketing organization in the foot." Control of prescription drug costs was not yet prominent in anyone's mind – except apparently mine. I disagreed with marketing, but initially that's all I could do. As CEO, however, I was at last in position to "persuade" my colleagues to try an experiment with generic drugs.

We'd be competing solely on the basis of price, which was not the traditional Merck way to do things. But if our customers wanted generic equivalents of our drugs, I thought we should be providing them.

In the early 1990s, we launched a generic drug business limited to Merck products no longer covered by a patent. This new policy put additional pressure on manufacturing to keep cutting costs, but that wasn't my major objective. My primary goal was to stay in touch with our customers and give them what they wanted and needed. That's why I persisted, listened to a great deal of grumbling, and finally shoved Merck into this low-margin business. I say "shoved" because my Merck colleagues continued for the most part to be dead set against this strategy.

Although generic drug manufacturing of Merck products was a minuscule operation at the start, the plan anticipated the expiration of patents on some of our most important products, including *Vasotec*, *Prinivil*, *Zocor*, and *Pepcid*, to mention only a few. Merck wasn't the first pharmaceutical company to sell its products in both a branded and generic formulation, but change at Merck came with particular difficulty because of the firm's long success with innovative, branded products.

\* \* \*

Despite the resistance, both internally and externally, to change, I thought by 1994 (when I was approaching mandatory retirement) Merck had made significant inroads on the pricing problem. We were getting into generic production, we had imposed limits on our own price increases, we had fought off an ill-planned attempt to introduce government price control, and we had pushed forward aggressively with vaccines, the most cost-effective means of preventing infections. Much remained to be done. But much had been accomplished.

# CHAPTER EIGHT

# Moral Leadership

T HE 1980S PROVIDED EVERY REASON TO THINK ALL business was corrupt. The newspapers were full of articles on
insider trading and Wall Street scandals. The most upsetting news
was about the gross profits made by people widely described
as financial parasites, people who sucked off billions of dollars
through complex schemes that most people had difficulty understanding. There were junk bond crazes and hostile takeovers by
financiers who broke up organizations instead of building them.
Much the same picture appeared on television, in local movie
theaters, and in popular magazines. Fiction, nonfiction, it was
all the same: People in business are not like you. They are fundamentally immoral, and the richest are making no positive contributions to our society.

Recently we have had another great burst of business scandals.
In the last few years some of the country's largest firms have collapsed as a result of corruption, leaving their shareholders, former
employees, and entire communities in deep distress. This time,
some of the leading firms in the accounting profession have been

caught up in the scandal for abandoning their watchdog role and approving the illegal practices of their corporate clients. Some of the largest banks are now paying off for their failure to alert their clients to the impending collapse of these corporations. Once again, men in powerful positions lined their own pockets while presiding over devastating collapses into bankruptcy.

My own experiences in the 1980s and early 1990s took place in an entirely different business world – one populated by people who were actually like most other Americans. And for that matter, like most people I've met around the world. I could see no difference in moral terms between my colleagues and competitors in business and the colleagues and competitors I'd known as a university administrator, scientist, and physician. In the university and in business, a few people were reasonable candidates for sainthood, and some were fundamentally immoral. But most were someplace in between, trying hard to do the right thing, to lead productive lives, and to make positive contributions to society. We weren't always succeeding – and yes, I place myself in that large middle group – but we kept trying. Here are some of the things we tried to do at Merck during those years.

* * *

One of our basic strategies was to anticipate and deal with situations before they became a source of political controversies and long before new government policies were imposed on Merck. The entire chemical industry – bulk chemicals, specialty chemicals, and pharmaceuticals – had a long history of creating environmental problems, often because the hazards were not initially understood by either the firms or the government. For more than a century, society had little scientific knowledge about how most chemical substances affect humans and other animals.

But gradually, researchers accumulated epidemiological evidence that pointed to particular substances as sources of disease. The environmental movement for the first time acquired a firm scientific foundation. We were no longer guessing about the need to impose limits on certain chemicals in order to maintain clean air, water, and soil.

The manufacturing wing at Merck, especially the chemical operations, had been working for many years to decrease the gases and chemicals released into the atmosphere or local waterways. For example, Merck had stopped dumping waste into the Atlantic Ocean long before that practice was prohibited. But when I returned to Rahway and the Merck Research Laboratories in the 1970s, my eyes and nose told me that the company still had a good bit to do on the environmental front.

Even before seeing the plume coming out of the TBZ (thiabendazole) plant, you could smell the mercaptans and other substances being wafted into the city. You could also detect a change in the weather by noting the intensity of the local smells, but back then, these byproducts seemed acceptable both to our people and to the local community. When I complained about the odors, the managers of the plant said, "You should be happy when you smell that. It means business is good. You should worry when you don't smell it." That was not a good answer for me.

I began to think about ways to improve Merck's procedures, but it was several years before I was in a position to take decisive action on that front. After I became CEO, the government sounded a wake-up call by publishing data on emissions of known or suspect carcinogens. Several chemicals that industry released in huge quantities into the environment were listed in the second category, the suspect carcinogens.

Merck was heavily involved in the production of organic substances – that is, our medicines – and some of the chemicals used
in our operations got us placed high on the government's list of
polluters. In Georgia, we were at the top of the list! There, a suspect carcinogen was critical in the production of an important
antibiotic. When we built the plant, there had been no reason to
worry about that chemical because its toxicity was not known.
Now it was known, or at least suspected, which was good enough
to persuade me to do something.

We decided to change our policies in two important regards.
First, we voluntarily established a specific target with a time
limit for the reduction of toxic emissions from our plants. We
announced this policy in 1989 with a target date of 1995. The
goal was to cut the environmental releases of the listed substances
by 90 percent – a formidable hurdle to clear. Some of the engineers
in our manufacturing division thought 40 percent would be more
reasonable. Even the Environmental Protection Agency wanted an
initial cut of only 50 percent. I doubt that any chemical company
in the world had adopted more stringent standards than these, and
it wasn't clear at first that we'd be able to achieve our objective.

We had more than forty plants operating around the world.
Some of the chemical manufacturing operations, like the TBZ
plant, were dedicated to a single product and had been running
for years. Now, suddenly, they were going to have to change
some important aspects of their operations, sometimes decisively,
because I had decided to cut emissions without any legal or political pressure to achieve the 90 percent goal. I knew this policy didn't make as much sense in Albany, Georgia, or Kilshee-
lan, Ireland, as it did in corporate headquarters, where we were
also pressuring manufacturing to cut costs while simultaneously

improving quality. The environmental initiative would be time-consuming and expensive: We initially estimated it would cost about $75 million.

I've always found that one of the hardest things to do in the corporate world is to encourage people to take risks and not stay in their current, comfortable situations. Many of Merck's chemical engineers were very talented. But they needed to be pushed. "How can we change our processes so that we no longer use a chemical like benzene?" we asked. Our engineers found a way to do it. In making our antibiotics, we used a solvent – methylene chloride – that we bought by the ton. "Let's get rid of methylene chloride," we said, and the first response was, "You've got to be kidding!"

But we kept the pressure on, and strong leadership in manufacturing combined with good engineering kept us going. Our chemical engineers came through even better than we expected. They eliminated the toxic substances *and* enabled us to cut the cost of production at the same time by completely reengineering the processes used to make some of our products. I was amazed. By 1993, we had hit the 65 percent level of reductions, and two years later, Merck crossed the 90 percent line. Rahway and several other sites around the world smelled better and were safer for both our workers and for the local residents.

Our second innovation was to make the new environmental program uniform for the entire world. Our plants in Ireland or Latin America would now have to meet the same standards as our factories in France, Japan, or the United States. The highest standard for any of the Merck sites became our global standard, regardless of any less stringent local or national regulations. All around the world, we pulled up all our underground tanks and stored everything above ground. Then, we put double piping in sewers so that we could see when a leak developed. Where we had evidence of past leaks, we cooperated with regulatory groups to ensure that the soil was not contaminated around our factories.

This policy, which made environmental sense, also made good business sense because it was consistent with the objectives of a company in the business of curing and preventing diseases. It positioned us at the forefront of the pharmaceutical industry and prepared Merck for the day, soon approaching, when high standards for the protection of the air, soil, and water will prevail all around the world.

We took the same approach to smoking cigarettes or cigars on Merck sites. How could a company dedicated to improved healthcare allow its employees to damage their health and the health of others while on the job? Years before, in my second month at Merck research, I had made my first move against smoking. I had all the ashtrays removed from the backs of the seats in the research auditorium. Some colleagues grumbled. But they realized I was serious about health risks in a health-dedicated company. Now, as CEO, I was really able to confront this problem.

Our policy was harsh. At Rahway, we didn't allow smoking even outside the buildings. Executives, managers, and all employees, from top to bottom, had to leave Merck property to smoke. They did, of course. There they were, huddled outside the gate, smoking in the middle of the winter. At Whitehouse Station, New Jersey, where we had built our new international headquarters, we had to make an exception to this rule. The wooded area around the large central building is so large it wasn't feasible to require smokers to leave the site. Instead, we constructed a shelter in the woods where they could smoke among the deer and geese.

Not surprisingly, these antismoking rules produced a great deal of distress. Our policy was international, and the French were especially vehement in opposition. But I wasn't about to waver on tobacco when our manufacturing organization was spending $75 million to eliminate other carcinogenic emissions.

During these same years, Merck universalized its quality controls and standards. We established a single worldwide standard for quality on every product. As with the environmental programs, we were positioning Merck for global competition over the long term. I thought both policies gave us a strong, forward-looking, competitive position while encouraging countries around the world to adopt the same high standards for all their pharmaceuticals. When they did, Merck would be ahead of the competition, moving at our own pace.

We followed the same logic when it came to safety in our plants – an area with which I had little direct experience. At NIH and Washington University, we had been very lax in handling dangerous substances, including radioactive isotopes. We sometimes went around the labs with glowing isotopes dancing along our arms. In the 1970s and early 1980s, however, stringent regulations were introduced in science laboratories, and at MRL we religiously followed all of the new rules.

The major safety problem wasn't in the labs but rather in manufacturing. There we were running large-scale, complex operations – some involving chemicals so volatile they could ignite merely by touching a warm surface. Our chief safety officer said our record for safety was "good but not great." Using statistical measures like the lost-time index, he evaluated our manufacturing plants around the world and compared our performance with the rest of the industry. According to his numbers, we were short of matching the performances of the leaders in industrial safety, but we'd made significant progress since the 1970s and now had safety professionals at every Merck manufacturing plant.

Still, we had a crisis in Barceloneta, Puerto Rico, in 1986. An explosion in one of our plants killed three people and injured others. After a careful study of this tragic situation, we were able to introduce new policies aimed at preventing similar problems in Puerto Rico and worldwide.

By 1994 we had uniform global policies on all these fronts – safety, quality, and environmental protection. We anticipated that, in future years, this explicitly international focus would enable Merck to avoid some crises and to deal from strength with governments around the world. In an industry at the forefront of globalization and with a high public profile everywhere, this would be no small advantage. Although some dividends from these policies might not be realized for many years – even decades – we were confident of a long-term payoff for Merck. In the meantime, we had helped to create the kind of enterprise with which we wanted to be associated.

\* \* \*

We also made progress in providing new opportunities for women and minorities. Was I influenced by my own origins and experiences in setting these policies? Of course. As the son of Greek immigrants, I was unusually sensitive to anything that smelled of privilege at the expense of performance. In my own family, I had seen what happened when young women, my sister Joan included, were guided toward marriage while young men, me included, were guided toward the advanced education and professional careers that are the bridge to success in our society. I wanted that bridge to be open to everyone smart enough to cross it and willing to do the hard work that waited on the other side. So I pressed for equal opportunity at Merck with unusual vigor.

In doing so, I was able to build on a solid foundation laid down long before I became CEO. In the 1970s, when the United States began to change national policies toward minorities and women, Merck had moved quickly to establish a strong position on what came to be labeled affirmative action. John Horan, my predecessor as CEO, had guided the development of Merck's aggressive program, which focused almost exclusively on African Americans and women. Under his leadership, management was so successful that one of the videos the company used to teach employees the standards Merck had adopted was purchased by several other companies and was actually employed by some government agencies trying to achieve the same goals. As CEO in the 1980s and 1990s, my job was to ensure that everyone in the company understood that we were dedicated to further progress on both these fronts.

Active recruiting was critical in increasing the number of African Americans working for Merck, and it took aggressive monitoring to keep them moving ahead at a brisk pace. We lost some superb candidates for top jobs when other firms offered them opportunities we didn't have available. Two who made the most of the opportunities they found at Merck were Brad Sheares and Ken Frazier.

Brad, a promising young scientist, had moved from Fisk University, a Black college, to Purdue for a Ph.D., then to MIT, and, following the usual postdoctoral fellowship, into the Merck Research Laboratories. He did a first-rate job at MRL, but after about five years of research, he came to see me. "Roy," he said, "I've got to talk to you." "What's the matter?" I asked. "I want to try something else," he said. I was stunned. He had been doing such a good job that we had been giving him more and more support, which in research means more and more people for his team. Off balance, I blurted out, "What are you talking about?" And he told me: "Roy, I know I can do research, but I'd like to try marketing." Further off balance, I said, "God, you must be crazy!"

But Brad, who was calmer than I was, explained, "I'd really like to try it. You see, my father was a preacher." That's all he had to say. I could see that he wanted to focus on people rather than research, and I saw him off into the marketing division with my corporate blessing and only a pinch of regret. By the time I retired as CEO, Brad was shooting up through marketing and sales. Subsequently, I learned that he had become president of Merck's U.S. Human Health division and just recently got another promotion. He is indeed his father's son.

Ken Frazier also came to Merck through the professions, but in his case the specialty was law. Harvard-trained, Ken was working for a distinguished Philadelphia firm that had long provided counsel to Merck, and we were able to persuade him to jump ship and become general counsel for our joint venture with the Swedish firm AB Astra. His combination of technical and people skills, energy, and self-discipline put him on the corporate fast track. He's completely open and honest, which are qualities extremely important to me. Veering away from law temporarily (under some pressure from his CEO), he became head of Merck's public affairs department. In 1999, I was pleased to see that he's moved back into law as the new head of the company's entire legal department. As a senior vice president and member of the Management Committee, he provides the kind of role model that aspiring young African Americans need at the same time that he's providing Merck's CEO with astute counsel.

The bridge these men took into the corporate world is the same one I crossed – an advanced professional degree. For African Americans, the journey through the educational system to that degree is always tougher. We recognized that at Merck, and we tried to help more African Americans down that road toward the professions most relevant to what we were doing. We began working with historically black colleges much as we had years before at Washington University. But this time we could provide some funding to about ten schools to encourage students who were studying science and mathematics. We hoped that in a few years some of these talented young Black scholars would come in the door at Merck ready to work with us.

Affirmative action is under fire today, but my experiences at Merck convince me that we will need these policies for another generation – perhaps more. I once met with a small group of African Americans to get an update on affirmative action at Merck from their perspective. I was surprised and saddened to learn that, in their opinion, an African American had to be 15 percent better than a White colleague to be promoted at Merck. I couldn't see this from my position at the top of the firm, but I believed them because they were intelligent, credible, sincere people. That's why I think our educational and corporate institutions must continue with forceful policies if we are ever going to achieve equality of opportunity for African Americans.

The situation with women was somewhat different. The pool of well-educated female university graduates and professionals was relatively large, and soon we were hiring about as many women as men in most divisions of Merck. Still, we had a twofold challenge. First, we had to make Merck stand out as the best place to work in order to attract the most talented members of this pool. Second, we had to ensure that opportunities for advancement would be available at all levels, including the very top, to keep our most successful recruits. Because women normally experience the tension between the demands of career and those of family and childrearing more acutely than men, it was important that we accommodate that situation.

It wasn't enough just to proclaim a level playing field and say that the best person, regardless of gender, would win. We had to provide good facilities for childcare, which we did at all our major locations. When we built our new international headquarters at Whitehouse Station, New Jersey, the architects designed a modern building, separated from the main offices, specifically for the purpose of childcare. We built a similar facility at Rahway and made other equally attractive arrangements at all of Merck's major sites. Flextime also helped both men and women employees juggle family and corporate responsibilities. We ensured that women who took pregnancy leaves would get their regular jobs back when they returned – a practice now required by law but not always honored by employers. When we made all these policies an integral part of our day-to-day operations, we had an organization that won a series of awards as one of the best places in corporate America for women to work.

The toughest barrier was the glass ceiling, a barrier evident in every large corporation with which I am familiar. I was determined to crack that ceiling at Merck, and I had been around the company long enough to know that I would have to crack a few hard heads as well. By 1989, more than half our new hires were women and almost 20 percent were minorities, but the Operating Review Committee – my top eight advisers – was still a White male preserve. The Management Council, a group of twenty-one in addition to me, included only one woman. I had been working on this problem since taking the helm as CEO, and I had a single woman in the second tier of the top executives to show for all my efforts.

Why was progress so slow? Of course, it took years for anyone to move through the ranks and become a president or senior vice president, and Merck had only begun its new policies on African Americans and women – a decisive break in corporate policies at the firm – in the 1970s. But that was just one part of the story.

Another aspect involved resistance to change on the part of some of our leading executives. The top management in any large institution tends to become a tightly knit community. That happened at Merck even though we had a considerable amount of turnover, which worked against solidarity. Nevertheless, the men running the company got to know each other extremely well, both on and off the job. Some had come up through the ranks together. Many shared an interest in golf, belonged to the same clubs, and dined together regularly. Although I never caught the golf bug, I loved to play tennis and sometimes played doubles with my fellow executives. We shared problems, interests, and the kind of chitchat about our families that fills the empty spaces in every organization's social life.

All these activities had a heavy male orientation that made it difficult for a woman to get accepted. Because most of my top executives had begun their careers before the 1960s, they were being forced to change some deeply grooved attitudes about gender roles in society. Like me, most of them had traditional marriages. A few were simply prejudiced against women, certain they couldn't deal with the pressures of the executive suite. Raised in an environment with two distinct tracks, one for men and one for women, they thought corporate leadership should remain a male preserve because it worked better that way. They weren't outspoken about these ideas. But I knew how they felt. Others – the majority – were simply comfortable with their current golf partners and convinced that all of their decisions about promotion were unbiased even when all the best jobs went to men. They believed in equal opportunity in the abstract but just weren't prepared to do anything about it in real life, that is, in their life.

To change this situation, I found a few unusually strong candidates for promotion to the Operating Review Committee. Mary McDonald had been with Merck's Legal Department since the mid-1970s under the tutelage of Robert Banse, our general counsel. She'd played an important role in handling discrimination and labor relations matters and had gained valuable experience with international operations. When Merck began to develop strategic alliances with other firms, such as Astra, Mary was a key player who helped keep the ball rolling when successful business negotiations had to be translated into sound contracts. With Banse's support, she was promoted to vice president and general counsel, becoming the second woman to join the eight-member Operating Review Committee. When Bob Banse retired, Mary succeeded him as head of the Legal Department, senior vice president, and my close adviser on all legal questions. I had complete confidence in her.

Nevertheless, I had to field the usual sorts of questions about the appointment. Although Mary is a strong, intelligent person with a firm grasp of the law, some colleagues suggested she might not be forceful enough for the top position. It was hard to tell exactly what this meant. It could have been a way of saying that women executives are generally not as aggressive as their male counterparts. It could have been suggesting that Mary, in particular, was too soft-spoken, too inclined to yield the floor, for us to make her a member of the club, the clique at the top. I just treated the opposition as if it were completely impartial and pushed the appointment through on the grounds that Mary had passed all of the tests and was the strongest candidate for the position.

When Mary McDonald joined the top group of Merck executives in 1992, the way had been paved by Judy Lewent, who had been elected vice president and chief financial officer in 1990. After graduating from Goucher College, Judy received an MBA in finance from the Sloan School at MIT and then worked briefly at Pfizer before moving to Merck. I had first worked with her as president of MRL, where she was controller, and had followed her career through the early 1980s, when her boss, Frank Spiegel, was coaching me on how to be a businessman.

Frank and Judy were a great combination: Frank was especially strong on accounting and the policy side of business, and Judy's strength was the analytical aspects of business finance and strategy. At the labs she developed a computer model that predicted the value of our projects right through product development and a successful launch. Her projections were very useful when I was dealing with corporate officers who had a better understanding of finance than they did of science. But Judy Lewent wasn't just some narrow technocrat. Her kind of analysis blended into business strategy and enabled the rest of us to make effective decisions involving long-range planning. It was evident to me and to others that Judy had CEO potential.

When we discussed promotions for Judy, even the most traditional of the Old Boys couldn't say she wasn't tough enough, not aggressive enough to handle one of the top rungs in the firm. Frank Spiegel, a Marine veteran, paid Judy the ultimate compliment he could offer. He said, "She'd make an excellent Marine officer!" I agreed. This made it easy for Frank and me, approaching retirement together, to ease Judy in as a senior vice president and heir apparent as CFO of a Fortune 50 U.S. corporation.

The only obstacles to the top job at Merck or another large corporation were her age and lack of operating experience. She had spent her entire career in a staff position, and to run a company like Merck, you normally need the sort of experience I had gained as executive vice president. In a more perfect world, I would have had more time before retiring to give her that experience, grooming her to vie for the position I was vacating. I was encouraged recently when Judy was able to get some line experience as a president of Merck's Human Health organization in Asia.

Did it make any difference that we added two women to the top rank of executives and that at least two African Americans were on target to join them in the future? I'm convinced that it did matter throughout the ranks at Merck, where women and minorities could see they wouldn't have to bump their heads on a gender or racial ceiling. It mattered to the company because it enlarged our pool of potential leaders and gave us a marginal advantage in recruitment. Every large corporation searches endlessly for managerial talent. Skillful, energetic risk takers who have solid technical backgrounds and can lead are always in short supply. By increasing and diversifying the supply, Merck had established a strong competitive position.

That was certainly true in Japan, where we had acquired the Banyu Pharmaceutical Company. Banyu had great difficulty recruiting top people as sales representatives because the top male university graduates preferred other industries. I wondered why they didn't use women for the positions. But I learned that in Japan sales reps traditionally took physician clients out for drinks and did other favors that wouldn't be appropriate for women. I agreed that some of those activities aren't appropriate for women, but I thought they weren't appropriate for men either.

As a result, we started a broad program at Banyu to retrain their representatives in the professional techniques used by Merck in every other part of the world. Once the men were working in this new style, we recruited women. By offering good professional jobs, we were able to recruit top Japanese women, who often performed better than the men. Banyu management was impressed by the women's performances, and within a few years women made up about 40 percent of their reps. Soon after, other Japanese pharmaceutical companies followed Banyu's lead.

\* \* \*

We had other opportunities to get ahead by doing the right things. You can find these opportunities if you will keep looking. One of our best business decisions earned us no profits in the twentieth century, but it promised to save more lives than anything else Merck has ever done. It furthermore may provide the company a strong position in the distant future in the world's largest national market. The decision involved *Recombivax HB*, our genetically engineered vaccine against hepatitis B. The market was the People's Republic of China, where the leading public health problem was infection by the hepatitis B virus.

The Chinese government approached Merck about transferring our technology for the production of *Recombivax HB* to their country. We were eager to do this and launched discussions with the People's Republic. Initially we wanted to sell our vaccine, but we quickly learned they could not afford it even at a much reduced price. So we then began to negotiate a technology transfer and found ourselves deeply mired in talks that promised to go on to the end of time. At least that's the way it looked to me in my anxiety to make a deal that would start saving children from a deadly viral infection.

The facts seemed clear. Our proposals were dirt cheap, but the discussions meandered as if no one were dying of liver cancer, no newborns were being infected, and no one needed to get around to making *Recombivax HB* in China. It drove me up a wall. I can be patient, although it takes an explicit effort once I think I understand a situation. But I was no match for the Chinese. My concept of long term included the first half of the twenty-first century. Their concept seemed to look beyond that to some epoch I couldn't even imagine.

Months dragged by, and so I finally decided to get something done. I told them we would charge a rock bottom price of $7 million and they could take it or leave it. Since I knew we would spend more than that to train the Chinese engineers and send Merck personnel back and forth to China, I thought this offer would quickly yield a contract. Well, they thought about the offer for another several months before accepting it.

Then, at last, the real work of technology transfer could begin. The Chinese sent a team from Beijing to West Point, Pennsylvania, bought all of the necessary equipment in the United States (it wasn't available in China), and assembled the processing equipment here under our supervision. After we helped them run several batches of the vaccine, they took the equipment apart and shipped it back to Beijing along with the crew that would run it. We sent the Merck chemical engineers who had trained them to assist in building the plant, assembling the equipment, and starting up the process. The two sets of engineers worked over a year putting together this splendid new stainless steel plant and getting it into production.

This episode also demonstrated to us how the Chinese Communists tried to create some of the benefits of American capitalist competition. They sent a second team of chemical engineers, from Shenzhen, about six months after the Beijing group arrived. Knowing they were behind in the race, our new guests asked if we could slow down their compatriots. "No, we can't do that," we said, "but we'll try to get you in operation as fast as we can."

We then repeated the entire process of helping them buy equipment, set it up, run it, dismantle it, and ship it to Shenzhen. We never learned how the team competition turned out, but we knew that China now had two state-of-the-art recombinant DNA vaccine plants capable of producing enough hepatitis B vaccine to immunize 20 million newborns each year. Just recently, I learned that they are now immunizing around 85 percent of each new birth cohort. Eventually, they'll be able to bring the disease under control, and when they do, I hope they will remember that Merck helped them save all those millions of lives.

\* \* \*

Sub-Saharan Africa, which also suffers massive public health problems, has even fewer resources than mainland China for treating or preventing disease. Some of the poverty-stricken nations of Africa can budget only a few dollars per year per person for public health, making the development of an effective health infrastructure impossible. Deadly infections like HIV/AIDS sweep over helpless populations with a loss of life reminiscent of the Black Death of the fourteenth century and the great influenza pandemic of 1918–19. Other debilitating diseases, including malaria and onchocerciasis, which causes river blindness, are endemic to the region.

As you saw in the first chapter, Merck and I had become involved with the river blindness puzzle as an unanticipated result of our discovery of ivermectin, which became the largest selling animal drug in history. My initial decision had been to send Bill Campbell and Mohammed Aziz off to get the information they needed before we had to make any more decisions. Would the drug work? Would there be damaging side effects?

Mohammed pushed very hard to get the information we needed. He started by discussing ivermectin with WHO parasitologists he knew and then launched initial studies in Dakar, Senegal. The results were positive. By this time, we had all seen the tragic pictures of African children leading blind adults, some of them very young, around their villages. With an acute sense of the need for a breakthrough therapy, we pushed ahead into expensive and complicated clinical trials that would tell us whether ivermectin would be safe and effective against this insidious parasite. We had to conduct the trials in African countries where onchocerciasis was endemic and where, unfortunately, the normal networks of professionals and health organizations that support clinical research didn't exist.

That's where our diversity came into play. Merck had an unusually high number of foreign nationals in very important positions, and we sought out foreign researchers in all of our non-U.S. research facilities. Our clinical research staff for this project was led by Aziz, an experienced traveler on jungle paths and unmarked trails.[1]

For Aziz – one of the few Merck researchers who knew anything about the disease – the new therapy, renamed *Mectizan*, became a crusade. Trips to Paris and Dakar, Senegal, yielded support for the first tests in humans. Coordinated through the University of Dakar, these initial studies were relatively simple. Infection was evident because the worms formed lumps in people's skin. Aziz and his crew took tiny skin snips from infected persons, counted the number of microfilariae, and then treated the people with the new

---

[1] Mohammed Aziz's own path to Merck had been far from normal. It began in Bangladesh, wound through college in Calcutta, to Dacca for a medical degree, and then to Minnesota, where he received a Ph.D. in clinical pathology. Further training at the Johns Hopkins School of Hygiene and Public Health was followed by study at the London School of Hygiene and Tropical Medicine. He was a coordinator for WHO in Sierra Leone, before moving to Merck.

drug. Testing the same way some weeks later, they were amazed to find that the microfilariae were all gone. Completely – with a single oral dose. When Aziz had confirmed the safety of the therapy in these patients and determined a proper dosage, Merck prepared to move ahead.

Aziz invited experts from WHO to review the results of the initial clinical study in Rahway. At that time WHO was running a large, expensive, modestly successful program of aerial spraying to suppress the black flies that spread the disease. Our researchers were convinced that *Mectizan* would be far more effective than spraying, but the WHO representatives were unenthusiastic about our experimental results. "Too preliminary to be meaningful," they said. "By testing more people, you'll probably get the usual drug-related side effects."

After that discouraging chat, Aziz and I had lunch with the WHO representatives. By the end of the meal, I was no longer discouraged. I was hot under the collar. But I admit to some prejudice because they all looked like bankers, wearing elegant suits and handcrafted neckties. This, I sensed, was a turf problem. I quizzed them about the expense and success rate of their spraying program, and they insisted their approach was problem free. They left expressing no interest in *Mectizan*.

That was all I needed to turn on a major Merck effort! I told Aziz he had all the resources he needed to find out how good *Mectizan* was and what its side effects would be. Aziz didn't need encouragement to get excited, and now he had the funds to mount a large, multinational clinical trial. After double-blind, placebo-controlled tests in Senegal, Mali, Ghana, and Liberia, followed by Phase studies, Aziz had solid evidence that oral *Mectizan* was safe, that it was far more effective than the current leading treatment (diethylcarbamazine), and that it needed to be taken only once a year.

As Aziz proceeded and the exciting results of his initial tests were discussed by infectious disease scientists, the WHO researchers returned to Merck and asked to participate. We eased their way back by suggesting that WHO should also continue its fly spraying and keep its air force aloft. But tensions continued. When WHO reported on tests of *Mectizan* conducted in its clinics, the organization sometimes failed even to mention Merck's involvement. I protested rather fiercely. They backed down, and we became good partners after that.

I followed the progress of Aziz and the clinical trials with great interest, but as CEO, I began to worry about the second part of the *Mectizan* puzzle. Even though a single annual, oral dose worked effectively, an organization had to exist to supply bottles of *Mectizan* for distribution in developing countries. Some of the countries with the greatest need did not have established healthcare delivery systems or even roads to the interior.

Who would pay for those bottles of the drug? We were already spending millions on this project, supplying both financial aid and the *Mectizan* for the trials. We were rapidly approaching a decision about production. Should we build a plant to produce the drug? If so, who would pay for it? We explored U.S. government support, but neither the U.S. Agency for International Development nor the Department of State had room in their budgets for a new program along these lines.

In 1987 we were left on our own. I'd had some practice with a similar issue in 1979, when Merck had considered closing its vaccine business. At that time, I'd helped keep us in vaccines, but with *Mectizan* the issue was drawn more sharply. There were only two possibilities. If we decided to sell *Mectizan*, it wouldn't reach those who needed it most regardless of how low we set the price. This was unacceptable for a company dedicated to improving human health. If, on the other hand, we decided to give it away, we would set a dangerous precedent for a pharmaceutical company that needed profits to sustain the sort of research and development that had made *Mectizan* possible. Giving *Mectizan* away would be expensive for Merck: At that time, 18 million people were infected, and 80 million more were at risk worldwide.

There were other complications to consider. Many in the developing world suffered from other virulent diseases, including malaria and HIV/AIDS. They would inevitably expect similar donations of medicines. By giving the drug away, we might discourage some organizations from developing new drugs for these and other diseases impacting the citizens of impoverished countries.

The decision was not obvious. We were now in a position to help millions of people. But I could not simply ignore my responsibilities as CEO of Merck. As I've already mentioned, we were under mounting pressure to control the prices of pharmaceuticals and were dealing with an unstable national political setting for healthcare issues. I was responsible for protecting the long-term future of the organization. I had to answer to the stockholders and our Board of Directors as well as to the employees and the communities in which they worked and lived. All of these thoughts were running through my mind, and they had to run through quickly.

I didn't have much time to ponder the alternatives. Suddenly, the French government informed Merck that it was about to approve the drug. We had gone to France for approval instead of the FDA because there was no river blindness in the United States. France had expatriates from its former African colonies living in Paris who had the disease and could participate in clinical tests. Our tests there were successful, and the government was prepared to move ahead at once.

As we hastily arranged a press conference in Washington, DC, I met with my staff and decided what Merck's position would be. There was no time to convene and consult with our Board. I reflected on my training as a physician and Merck's mission statement: "to provide society with superior products and services." *Mectizan* was an incredibly effective medicine that could improve the lives of millions of people around the world. It was deliverable – it took one dose a year to do its work, not, say, three doses a day on a strict schedule.

I decided Merck would give the drug free to any person endangered by river blindness anywhere in the world for as long as it was needed. That was what I announced to the press. We would, of course, work through organizations capable of distributing the drug to the endangered populations. Shortly after that, the Board convened and was completely supportive. But there was a tense moment or two before I explained why I had been willing on my own authority to commit Merck's resources ad infinitum to the fight against river blindness.

The next step was to create an independent committee of experts to decide which distribution programs qualified for supplies of the drug. As you might imagine, this humanitarian initiative attracted an array of outstanding volunteer experts. Former President Jimmy Carter and his wife Rosalyn were very supportive and, in 1994, they accompanied Diana and me on a visit to a village in Chad when the second annual dose of our drug was being administered in that country. We arrived on foot. Even our Land Rover couldn't make it into this part of central Africa.

The trip was moving – unforgettably so. The heat, the flies, and the mud huts without electricity or running water were overwhelming. So was the presence of so many blind people, old and young. We saw a blind seventeen-year-old mother suckling her infant. *Mectizan* couldn't restore her sight, but happily it could protect her baby from river blindness. Equally unforgettable was the people's excitement upon meeting an American President.[2]

Over the next ten years, we delivered more than 96 million treatments. Some villagers walked for three days to reach a distribution point. In 1997 alone (the tenth year of the program), between 19 million and 20 million people received *Mectizan*, largely through ministries of health and nongovernmental organizations. In 2004 a total of 45 million people were being treated for river blindness, and the number increased every year.

River blindness is likely to be eradicated after a decade or so of further treatments – much like smallpox. Only humans are hosts for the parasite. If most people in a large region are treated with *Mectizan*, all the microfilariae will be eliminated, and the black flies (which transmit this infection) will have no source for the parasite. The disease cycle will end. To my knowledge, this would be the first example in history of a company contributing a drug to eradicate a disease.

---

[2] When the first dose had been administered, I was told, Chadians had been suspicious of the pill. "Why," they asked, "should we take a medicine that no Americans are taking?" But after a few people took the pills, stopped itching, and passed dead worms in their stools, the doubters were persuaded. The dead worms, unrelated to river blindness, had been living in their intestines as parasites, but they too were killed by *Mectizan*.

Is Merck's *Mectizan* donation program wise corporate policy? The plan eventually cost Merck over $200 million.[3] The company has made many other donations through the Merck Company Foundation, including a very large grant to build the Children's Inn (for families of children suffering from cancer) at the National Institutes of Health and gifts to universities (including Harvard and the University of Pennsylvania) and hospitals (Massachusetts General Hospital, among others). Some argue that corporations should not be in the business of making donations, contending that their sole obligation is to reward their stockholders with higher dividends and not squander company resources on gifts.

I strongly disagree. Corporations, no less than individuals, need to be good citizens and should be held to a high moral standard. Our policy on *Mectizan* and other gifts made Merck a place where people were proud and excited to work because they wanted to make lives better around the world. It helped us recruit the best people and build company morale. It was consistent with Merck's fundamental corporate philosophy of doing well by doing good. It served the global society Merck serves. It also served Merck's stockholders because corporate social generosity is often followed by higher profits as the corporation becomes a better, more attractive workplace for the best talent.

My only regret about the *Mectizan* program involves its timing. We couldn't launch the first donations until we solved all the organizational problems. By then, Dr. Mohammed Aziz had succumbed to stomach cancer. He was able to attend the Washington

---

[3] After my retirement, I was encouraged to see Merck expanding its *Mectizan* donation program to cover elephantiasis (lymphatic filariasis, which also has a microfilarial stage), a parasitic disease affecting millions in Africa. By 2004, 25 million persons were being treated with *Mectizan* for lymphatic filariasis.

THE MORAL CORPORATION

press conference in October 1987, when we announced our donation policy, but he died just as the first delivery of *Mectizan* was
being completed. He will never be forgotten by those still working
to eradicate the scourge of river blindness.

\* \* \*

So where does Merck fit in the moral array of the hundreds of thousands of companies in all lines of business in the United States?
Or in a similar, much larger array for the entire world? Objective, systematic comparisons of corporate social responsibility are
impossible because no one knows very much about most of these
organizations. Every business day the firms on the New York Stock
Exchange, NASDAQ, and the American Stock Exchange all get
graded by the market, which sets a price for their stocks. But only
a few are evaluated for moral behavior, and that's usually done
on the front page of your local paper, the *New York Times*, or the
*Wall Street Journal*. When they do make the front page, it's usually
bad news for the company and its employees.

Merck & Co., Inc., became big news in the 1980s and 1990s
for the first time in its long history. The profits from those billion-
dollar drugs we were rolling out attracted attention as did our
innovations in pricing policy and even some of the unusual things
we did like donating *Mectizan*. The firm won several awards for
its environmental and employee policies and was elected seven
years in a row as *Fortune's* Most Admired Corporation. Judging
from that evidence, Merck was by the time of my retirement on
the right side of our moral bell curve, right at the top of the good
guys.

Pleasing as that might be to Merck people, I'm not satisfied with that answer. The policies we followed in the 1980s
and early 1990s were, I thought, consistent with Merck's

guiding philosophy in the 1970s, when the company was not yet big news. We frequently reminded people inside and outside the firm what George W. Merck, the founder's son and company leader from 1925 until 1957, said about the Merck mission: "We try never to forget that medicine is for the people. It is not for the profits. The profits follow, and if we have remembered that, they have never failed to appear." He and Merck faithfully followed those guidelines. But most of what Merck did for many years wasn't big news and wasn't noticed, even though it was indeed moral behavior.

What we had at Merck in the 1980s and 1990s was a series of special opportunities – some related to medical science, some to economic performance, and some to what we might call social responsibility. We vigorously and effectively took advantage of those opportunities and that attracted the attention of the media. We were quick to respond to the unusual situations developing in the medical sciences, especially in enzymology and then in molecular genetics. We implemented a business strategy appropriate to our changing markets and the national and global economies. We were also vigorous and innovative about our social responsibilities. But remember, we didn't create the medical sciences, nor did we shape the national and international political economy in which Merck thrived. Absent those two settings, few would have noticed that we were, indeed, a moral corporation.

Why am I so certain about that? Because I am now chairman of two small start-up firms. I'm the same person I was before I retired from Merck in 1994. Both companies are focused on producing products needed by patients in the United States and around the world, and both have the same moral standards that George W. Merck expressed so eloquently. Neither company is front-page news – yet – nor do many people know anything about them.

But both of these companies are, I believe, close to the norm in moral terms for American business. Although our business system is far from perfect, it has long been the most successful in the world. Headlines notwithstanding, our high moral standards have contributed to that success.

# CHAPTER NINE

# Afterwards

When I retired in 1994, I left Merck with several major regrets. One was completely personal. Company policy required me to stop doing what I loved, and I found that very upsetting. Love is the right word in this case. I loved the opportunity I had to play a role in building a successful pharmaceutical company, and I hated the thought of retirement. After a brief interlude in which I was introduced to depression for one of the first times in my adult life, I found a number of new problems to solve and new opportunities to help improve our society.[1]

My second regret was that I was never completely satisfied with the level of innovation we had achieved in our marketing efforts. Although Medco had made tremendous strides in lowering the costs of distribution, the old system of personal "reps" remained intact and continued to play a large role at Merck and throughout

---

[1] Readers who have an interest in these problems and opportunities should consult Chapter 12 of P. Roy Vagelos and Louis Galambos, *Medicine, Science, and Merck* (Cambridge, 2004).

the rest of the industry. We had introduced laptop computers and emphasized the role our reps played as sources of up-to-date information for physicians and other healthcare professionals. We had the highest standards in the industry, I believe, for what we would say about our products and those of our competitors. But the system was still fundamentally flawed.

We sent our well-trained reps to wait in physicians' offices for hours hoping to spend a few precious minutes with the doctor. When I was a practicing physician, many years ago, I never talked to reps because I didn't want to waste my time. So you can see how conflicted I was. As CEO at Merck, I had for years presided over a system I knew was inefficient. I also knew, however, that if a drug company didn't market its products aggressively, using the traditional approach, it could not maximize sales. At least not under existing market conditions.

We experimented with some new approaches, but we failed to find a successful alternative to the current, wasteful system. Information technology, and in particular the Internet, may ultimately be the answer, but in recent years, all of the large firms – Merck included – have moved in the opposite direction. They have ramped up their sales forces, sending out new cadres of reps to deliver samples, gifts, and pizzas in return for a few moments with the doctor.

Even more disappointing to me was the problem of developing my successor. One of the most important responsibilities for any CEO is to prepare for an orderly succession, normally by grooming an heir apparent. I had done just that at MRL. And as CEO, I had begun identifying and developing potential successors long before others were thinking about and gossiping about my retirement. All went well, and the Board of Directors and I were anticipating a smooth transition.

But at a late moment in the process, my plan crashed when our lead candidate left Merck for personal reasons. The Board launched a search that began by reviewing the firm's top executives and continued with a survey of business leaders outside of Merck. They selected Ray Gilmartin, who was then heading Becton-Dickinson, a medical equipment firm. Although Ray had no experience in pharmaceuticals, he was a talented business strategist with a special ability to encourage a cooperative approach to any business activity.

Once Gilmartin had taken over and the transition was completed, I stepped aside. I resigned from the Merck Board of Directors, although I was urged to stay on the Board and remain involved with the firm. I didn't want to sit on the Board, however, and suggest to the new CEO and others in the company that I was looking over their shoulders, being critical of what they were doing as new problems developed.

* * *

New problems abounded. Not just for Merck, but for the entire industry. One of the central issues was the declining rate of new drug development. This had happened before and will happen again. Merck recruited me in the 1970s to help the firm get out of a flat phase of innovation when medicinal chemistry, pharmacology, and traditional random techniques were no longer producing breakthrough drugs. The flat phase was industrywide then, just as it is now.

Very few of the professionals who stay up with the science base of the industry believe that this will be a permanent condition. The advances in molecular genetics, in virology, and in advanced research techniques have laid the foundation for another spurt in new drug development. Our understanding of diseases and of the means of disease prevention and cure forecast a positive future for mankind and for the pharmaceutical industry. The special American combination of small-firm, biotech innovators and large firm producers and distributers will have a great deal to do with that positive outcome.

Unfortunately, however, for the large pharmaceutical firms trying to get through the current flat phase in innovation, their industry has experienced one of the most remarkable declines in public favor in modern history. Let me briefly chart my perception of this astonishing fall from grace. It all began with success, not failure, in new drug development.

Crucial to the setting was the great HIV/AIDS pandemic, a public health crisis with no known solution.[2] In the age of modern scientific medicine, this new plague seemed to have returned us to the epoch before sulfa drugs, penicillin, and the new viral vaccines had transformed medical practice. Once again, physicians were helpless to prevent or cure a disease that in its final stages killed virtually every person who was infected. The disease hit with devastating results in the 1980s, spread in the 1990s, and in 2004, when close to 40 million people were living with the virus, it was estimated to have caused over 3 million deaths worldwide.

In 1986, Merck had embarked on a major HIV research effort. This was risky because the virus had only been identified in 1983. Much basic research remained to be done. But the HIV/AIDS pandemic was too threatening to wait for basic science to make its discoveries. We moved ahead knowing that MRL would need to

[2] AIDS (acquired immunodeficiency syndrome) is a late stage in the development of an HIV (human immunodeficiency virus) infection. The virus attacks the body's immune system, ultimately weakening it to such an extent that the patient succumbs to secondary infections of various sorts.

do a significant amount of basic research as well as the normal applied research.

At Merck we were looking for either a vaccine to prevent infection or an antiviral drug that would effectively treat the infection. Neither Merck nor the rest of the industry was able to discover a vaccine that would work, but Merck and other firms were able to develop a number of antivirals that inhibited the enzymes crucial to viral replication. This work was well underway as I was retiring. In brief, the new drugs enabled physicians to control the infection but not get rid of it.

For those with advanced AIDS, the new antivirals were literally their lifesavers. The regimens were demanding and the drugs were expensive, but they worked. Resistance was still a major problem. But the new antivirals in the 1990s sharply reduced the mortality from HIV infections.

But this happened at first only in the developed nations where patients and their private or public insurers could afford the new drugs and the healthcare infrastructure could support the patients. In many parts of Africa, Latin America, and Asia, neither patients nor their governments could afford the new drugs. The result was a drumbeat of criticism of the greedy pharmaceutical companies that would not reduce their prices. They valued their patents and profits, the critics said, more than they did the lives of those suffering from HIV/AIDS.

The major pharmaceutical companies – "big pharma" in the media – responded to the pandemic in the developing world. As early as 2000, Merck was helping to launch a new public-private HIV/AIDS program in Botswana and working toward the establishment of lower prices for developing nations. But the industry was moving too slowly and with too many missteps that provided ammunition to the industry's critics. Pressure mounted after a firm in India began to sell generic versions of the HIV drugs in Africa at very low prices. Merck's public–private partnership with the government of Botswana and the Bill and Melinda Gates Foundation has been successful, but by the time these new policies and programs started to gain a secure place in the industry's public image, the media campaign against big pharma was being translated in the United States into a political movement. Prices were again a central issue. An aging population, a large number of citizens without medical insurance, and an industry that was increasing prices faster than the rate of inflation combined to produce a forest fire of new criticism. A few firms stoked the flames by charging outlandish prices for particular new drugs.

The attacks steadily mounted. Mergers and acquisitions created ever larger targets for the opponents to assault, and the industry's heavy investments in marketing and sales undercut the business argument that high returns were needed to fund advanced R&D. Accounting scandals and the recent wave of concern about the safety of vaccines and prescription drugs left pharmaceutials vulnerable to political attacks at the state and federal levels of our government. It has seemed of late as if the industry was writing a prescription for its own demise.

The major threat to its future in the United States comes from the advocates of price controls. This is not a new issue. It has come up before and will come up repeatedly in the future, making it difficult for the industry to defend a form of public–private partnership that has sustained the most innovative medical, scientific, and pharmaceutical establishments in the world's history. Inevitably, price controls will over the long term dampen innovation. No careful student of the collapse of centrally controlled economies would, I believe, advocate price controls as a means of improving new drug development. It is no accident that most of the world's most important new drugs have in recent decades come from the U.S. industry.

Before we introduce price controls, I hope we will reflect on the fact that our vast complex of partnerships has enabled millions of people to improve the quality of their lives and saved the lives of many additional millions throughout the world. Personally, I am grateful for the opportunities I have had – as a practicing physician, a research scientist, a university administrator, and a senior executive of one of the world's leading pharmaceutical companies – to play a role in making that system work. I believe it has a great future if everyone who cares about medical progress will study carefully the sources of our past success.

# Index

# INDEX